The Quantum Being

A Self-Sustaining and Magnificent Human Craft

Self-Ignite to Launch Your Magickal Life

Shehnaz Soni

Ashes to Sona: An Alchemist,
on a Transformational Journey!

Foreword by Sacha Stone

eBook ISBN: 978-1-958405-17-8
Paperback ISBN: 978-1-958405-18-5
Hardcover ISBN: 978-1-958405-19-2
Library of Congress Control Number: 2022916919

Foreword: Shehnaz Soni
Cover: Krunal Patel
Interior Design: Marigold2k
Publisher: Spotlight Publishing House - Goodyear AZ
https://spotlightpublishinghouse.com

For information, contact Shehnaz Soni at 281-804-0930.

www.shehnazsoni.com

The Quantum Being

A Self-Sustaining and Magnificent Human Craft

Self-Ignite to Launch Your Magickal Life

Shehnaz Soni

Goodyear, Arizona

I have known Shehnaz Soni as a work colleague at NASA's Marshall Space Flight Center for four years. We became close friends over this time. You will discover in reading this book that Shehnaz is a fierce seeker of knowledge. She is admired by all her co-workers as an articulate aerospace engineer. I so admire the ability she has to put into print her very personal experiences of seeking and discovering a more fulfilling life. She is full of enthusiasm. She is a woman who is as beautiful inside as the beautiful woman you see. It is amazing to read of a woman facing so many life challenges and continually choosing paths which bring her into victorious living. She has turned her "ashes into gold". She is truly a "life coach". A woman of "true grit" who takes irritations of life and makes pearls of them.

-Kenny Mitchell
Kenny Mitchell Retired NASA Engineer and Author

Thank you, Shehnaz, for holding courage and sharing your story in a way that entices one's consciousness into the realm of "infinite possibilities". Your words will surely encourage a multitude of souls to dream of a future today worthy of our divine existence.

-Holley Kushniryk
Holley's entrepreneurial spirit as a "Jill of all trades" has positioned her to work, travel, connect, love, and live with vitality, and humor.

Wonderful masterpiece Shehnaz, captivating and very well written, you may have a new calling in writing. Having met you in person and getting to know you and where you are now make me appreciate how one can overcome and prevail despite many struggles and obstacles in life, the like of which you endured and conquered. Hats off to you and big kudos for a wonderful and enthralling book, many will truly be inspired.

-Santos Bonacci, A Master Syncretism
Santos Bonacci is a longstanding researcher in the fields of Astrology, religious symbolism, and alchemy, weaving these threads and many more into a perspective called Syncretism

"Shehnaz Soni is a Light Being of a Rare and Most Pure Spirit and Intention! Her insights will envelop you with Love, Understanding and open New Doorways to your Inner Self!"

-David Sereda, Light stream Harmonics
David Sereda is a Canadian musician, singer, actor, playwright, pianist and composer. He is a frequency guru per Sacha Stone. We became friends working together supporting Lazarus Initiative with Sacha Stone.

Quantum Being finds answers to the questions of the metaphysical through the lens of quantum mechanics. By interweaving her life experiences with her advanced engineering background, Shehnaz Soni has written a book that can positively affect even the most complicated of life's challenges.

-Dr Bryan Wylie, Chiropractor

Contents

Dedications

The people whom I believed in

I would like to acknowledge all creation and the Creator who has filled my life with loving and encouraging friends and family. I am grateful for an amazing life and aspirations that grow inside my heart and open new doors to love, transformational experiences, and constant evolution. I am grateful for an incredible career where I am helping humanity explore the Moon and Mars, and I look forward to the day we can all be part of Cosmic and Galactic Level Federations, working with other species as we experience life as shown in the *Star Trek*-drama series, where society puts value to your passion and skills, not money.

I am grateful for the men who came into my life and taught me to be strong. First and foremost, my dad was pivotal in my transformation from ashes to gold, a journey to becoming a woman of substance. I am grateful for my dad, whom I miss immensely, and I send my love to him as he waves at me among the stars. Relationships are not always smooth sailing. However, as we emerge from the storm, our bond gets stronger, and our character builds resilience that becomes our best tool for life. By providing resistance to my relentless pursuits, my dad made sure that my inner fire burned bright and steady. I am grateful for my two ex-husbands, whom I compare to my dad. They continued the role-playing of providing resistance in my path, so I was galvanized and able to emerge as a strong leader.

I am in awe as a mother of four beautiful, intelligent boys who have been my four pillars and taught me about the limitations and strengths we carry as human beings. My boys have helped me learn lessons in patience and humility by continually challenging me to prove my spiritual concepts. Those challenges led me to the scientific research referenced in this book.

I am grateful for my oldest son, who taught me patience and belief in faith versus fact. By age 25, I had seen so much adversity that I didn't think there would be any more heartaches in my life. So, when we went to our seventh monthly well-baby visit for my oldest son, I was surprised when the pediatrician requested an MRI due to his limitation in hand movement. The doctor explained to us that the damage was severe, and there was no telling if he would be able to walk, talk, or have any kind of normal life. The doctor's prognosis devastated me.

Being a rebel, standing up for my truth, and not allowing others to define my destiny are all immutable aspects of my soul signature. Therefore, I decided I would stay the course and give my son the best possibility for a better outcome and a better life, no matter the prognosis. I remember teaching him simple tasks such as how to put his socks on; it required every ounce of my patience. Later, though, he persevered through multiple surgeries, mockery from kids at school, and all sorts of physical limitations. His tenacity and hard work paid off, and today he has graduated from Calhoun Community College in the field of robotics and mechatronics with a 3.8 GPA. He is currently enrolled at the University of South Alabama, pursuing his lifelong passion of becoming a meteorologist.

THE QUANTUM BEING

I have attracted angels and friends everywhere I go on this extraordinary planet where I live. These quantum beings always showed up when I needed them and brightened my day and life, creating radically new Realities.

Acknowledgment

The people who believed in me!

When we show up for each other, as quantum beings, we magnify our power and create miracles. I would like to honor the following people who have always believed in me and encouraged me to author this piece of art, a culmination of a lifetime of experiences as a quantum being.

I am grateful for my mom, a beautiful soul whom I have often challenged due to my different way of embracing life. She has always loved me despite our differences. Our relationship is mostly remote due to being a continent apart; however, I am closer to her than anyone else in my life due to our kindred spirits.

I am grateful for my friend, Holley Kushniryk, who has been there for me as a friend to lean on, have fun with, and bounce around ideas on life, death, and our spiritual journey beyond. I am thankful for my friend, Jane Reed, who guided me through some tough physical challenges. Numerous times in my life, I was extremely sick and had no one to look after me. She insisted that I go to the doctor or the hospital, which saved me in critical situations. I appreciate my friend Linda Hileman who offered her unconditional love whenever I needed it, through sickness and health.

ACKNOWLEDGMENT

I am grateful to my friend, Kenny Mitchell, who inspired me to write this book. Kenny is a published author passionate about seeking the truth about our human existence and origin. He came into my life right at the cusp of waking to my divine mission. I met him on September 4th, 2018, when I started working for NASA. His vast knowledge and exuberance reminded me of my dad in many ways: a great communicator, full of enthusiasm, and exuding passion even at the age of 80.

Lastly, and most importantly, I am thankful for Jessica Olma at Scribe Syndicate and her team of editors. Without them, this book wouldn't have made it into your hands and mine. There cannot be better people to edit this book than my target audience avatars. They are direct representations of the people I hope to attract through this book.

Foreword

By Sacha Stone

"In everyone's life, at some time, our inner fire goes out.
It is then burst into flame by an encounter with another
human being. We should all be thankful for those
people who rekindle the inner spirit."

-Albert Schweitzer

What better time to depart the myth of time than right here, right now? What deeper space might we hope to explore than the limitless expanse of our "innerverse," a vast and boundless horizon of inexhaustible creativity and expansion, genius and revelation?

Where better to begin this odyssey toward the actualization of immanence and perfection than with the next footstep we choose to take upon this plane of mortal existence? For it is the choice we make in the embodiment of now that the tapestry of noble destiny reveals upon the canvas of life—indicating an apocalypse…or ascension.

This measure of Reality renders upon the collective as it does upon the individual. The great 21st-century shroud of covidiocy from which we emerge is a testament to that resounding fact. The absence of a relationship with self is a choice and one that engages the laws of fractality to the great detriment of our human soul. Every moment contains the majesty of all of creation across all dimensions of Reality.

So then... how do we return to self? How do we reconvene alpha and omega? How do we rekindle immanence? Where do we conceive the unknowable? How do we speak the ineffable? When do we stop interminable seeking?

By doing so—is the answer.

Shehnaz Soni is both navigator and pilot in the abstruse arena of reckoning with self. She takes the diminutive to the capitalized and the linear to the quantum. She explores the question while divining the answer.

She does so because she is equipped to do so. She does so because she embodies the alchemical processes of transmutation and transcendence within the storyline of her own journey.

She does so because she is purposed to do so in this world at this time.

Listen closely...

Sacha Stone
Bacalar, Mexico
April 29, 2022

Founder of the International Tribunal for Natural Justice, The New Earth Project, and the New Earth Horizon, Promoter of Conscious Living.

Preface

"Man cannot discover new oceans unless has the courage to lose sight of the shore."
-Andre Gide

I have been an open-book personality since birth. My exchanges with people, places, and everything around me have always been rich. My capacity to tell a story is natural. Consequently, from time to time, I have been directed by others to write a book.

My book has come about over time. Living my life for half a century in this quantum body has gifted me the wisdom to navigate life with a strategy beneficial for the natural progression of life and its universal laws.

The universe runs on seven natural laws. The seven laws are sprinkled throughout the book and summarized below:

1. The principle of mentalism
2. The principle of correspondence
3. The principle of vibration
4. The principle of polarity and duality

5. The principle of rhythm
6. The principle of cause and effect
7. The principle of gender

My book offers insight into my life and my personal experiences that have led me to be who I am to date: an accomplished aerospace engineer, an effective transformational coach, a powerful spiritual healer, and a mother. My life experiences, or life essences, have included both unhappy and happy memories, many babies, numerous diseases, and countless cultural, religious, and spiritual shocks—and yet, I survived. We can take what happens to us and make it a source of our happiness by transforming our challenges into solutions.

This book is a combination of personal story sharing and wisdom designed to help others learn from my experiences to enhance their lives. While "Quantum Being" offers both spiritual and scientific points of view, I do not provide scientific proof for everything I believe in because spirituality precedes science.

As we launch our human craft to take flight into our Magickal life, we do this in three separate journeys.

1. Flight One: Soul Recognition
2. Flight Two: Soul Awakening
3. Flight Three: Soul Activation

Initially, I recommend reading the chapters in chronological order since each understanding is built on the other, like rungs on a ladder. Later on, you can use this book as a tool and, depending on your current life situation, revisit the chapter to remind yourself of the messages that speak directly to you.

Flight One: Soul Recognition

In Chapters 1 to 4, I shed light on my personal journey as an immigrant to the United States and how I overcame the life situations and cultural and language barriers that prepared me to be here with you right now.

Chapter 1 - Inner Fire:
I become aware of my inner fire going through my journey from childhood to adulthood, being born during the war, raised in a patriarchal society, and experiencing religious-induced sexual trauma. I channeled all that energy into a personal quest to move forward to my dream life without being sucked down the path of victimhood.

Chapter 2 - Riding the Wave:
My arrival to the U.S. as an immigrant came right after an arranged marriage. I had to ride the waves of change like a tenacious surfer to become acclimated despite significant cultural and language barriers. The principle of rhythm is the key to this chapter.

Chapter 3 - Golden Cage:
Like a forest bird, I flew away from the expectation embedded in me since childhood. The beliefs surrounding what it meant to be a good Muslim, a good daughter, a good wife, and a good mother to qualify for Heaven on judgment day.

Chapter 4 - Mobius Strip:
Our belief in following the most popular perceptions of success and family life can keep us in the infinite loop of the Mobius strip. How do we recognize our participation in this loop and create a successful exit plan?

We establish a connection in these early chapters and can begin a deep dive into discovering wisdom through unpacking ancient, mystical, scientific, and spiritual teachings.

Flight Two: Soul Awakening

In Chapters 5 to 8, I share how my self-reflection became a journey that allowed me to be true to my soul. By doing so, I share how we can all find an inner peace within ourselves.

Chapter 5 - Being Human:
To make the most out of life, we have to be in a state of quantum being, moment to moment, by understanding the fractal nature of existence and how it creates a self-repeating pattern of cause and effect.

In a state of quantum being, we affect our quantum manifestation every nanosecond. The axiom "as above, so below" in the principle of correspondence, and the principle of cause and effect are the key to this chapter.

Chapter 6 - Mirror, Mirror:
Our childhood fairy tales groomed us to look outside for validation. We are the common denominator in all of our relationships. How do we comprehend ourselves and our reflected self so we can exit the pattern of attracting people with the same unhealthy habits?

Chapter 7 - Weaver Within:
Energy is at the heart of everything we experience. We are weaving these energies with our thoughts, frequency, and vibration. The principle of mentalism is the key to this chapter, emphasizing that what we hold in our thoughts and minds will become our Reality. The principle of vibration is another natural law that weaves our Reality.

Chapter 8 - Intelligent Architecture:

Who is the ultimate choreographer of our universe? What is the morphogenetic field? How does everything become matter out of energy? How does sacred geometry play a vital role in what we see? Sacred geometric patterns in the form of the Flower of Life and Jacob's ladder exist all around us, creating the fundamental structure and templates of life in the universe. The principle of polarity, along with the principle of gender, is intertwined in the duality we experience every day in all forms.

Flight Three: Soul Activation

In Chapters 9 to 12, I highlight the secret recipe for manifestation through the journey within, so you can find the secret to making your life match your dreams.

Chapter 9 - Step into Your Light:

I explain how we see everything through a very narrow electromagnetic spectrum of light. Light defines how we perceive everything around us. Light and time are interwoven, and we are light beings. We need to leverage this understanding to brighten the journey through darkness and towards manifestation.

Chapter 10 - Quantum Universe:

We live in a quantum universe where observation affects momentum and interference affects our Reality. These concepts are the foundation for quantum manifestation. "How we manifest" matters as much as "what we manifest." This means what gets you here keeps you here.

Chapter 11 - Conscious Evolution:

To evolve consciously, we must understand what an illusion is, what is real, and how the holographic universe plays a key role in our evolution. We are the conduit in everything we experience, and we are also affecting all we experience based on our consciousness and self-awareness.

<u>Chapter 12 - Magickal Spark:</u>

In this book's last chapter, the rubber meets the road. Here you get your "Magickal formula" to make manifestation happen daily. By taking small steps each day, you can make life Magickal and have fun living life as a quantum being.

NOTES:

- ➢ The word Magickal is misspelled deliberately as part of my Mystery School teachings.
- ➢ Quantum physics versus quantum mechanics are all the same in this context.
- ➢ The word Reality is capitalized since it is a focus of this book and highlights the concepts better.

THE QUANTUM BEING

Prologue

As we undertake the daunting task of transformation, we embark on the journey that will ultimately become habitual, automatic, and effortless – akin to a rocket leaving the Earth. At first, the initial launch requires enormous power, then less and less as it leaves the Earth' gravitational field. Finally, the rocket moves through space and under its own momentum breaking all barriers, beyond imagination to traverse new worlds.

-Shehnaz Soni

*A*ll my life, I have worked hard to comprehend my existence, consciousness, and role-playing in this enormous universe. Why? Because without the quest to understand ourselves, life is meaningless. This quest to seek, learn, explore, and comprehend everything around me is what excites me to wake up every day. I would rather live with my divinity than live without it.

We must understand the fact that we are wearing an Iron Man outfit in the form of a human craft – as a human being. Our soul is woven into the human craft, making us magnificent quantum beings. We are self-sustained and powerful superhumans capable of launching our Magickal life.

My trip to Egypt in 2019, visiting the Great Pyramids and other sacred sites

"Everything that we need is inside of us!" This message was reinforced during my visit to Egypt in October 2019. I traveled to this magnificent country to explore truth in a place that holds spiritual and technological information about our origin and destiny. When we visit sacred sites, we exchange energies and remind ourselves how incredible we are as quantum beings. Exploring Egypt reminded me of my childhood in Karachi, Pakistan, due to the similarities in the countryside, people, cultural essence, cuisine, and hospitality.

Everything I have ever wanted is all here with me now! Isn't it ironic that I have been searching for me, to find missing pieces of the puzzle, all my life? It took me a while to realize that there were no missing pieces. I have been wearing the ruby slippers to go home all along, like Dorothy in "The Wizard of Oz." In every single superhero movie, we hear the same message over and over again.

The power we seek is the power within.

We, humans, are technological marvels. We are a magnificent innovative craft. We are the tools, gadgets, and light beings in the form of quantum beings, who can find our way back home. What is best suited for you is that which brings you more joy, peace, fun, and happiness and helps you:

Be the dreamer and the dream,
Be the creator and the creation,
Be in the world, but not of it.

I saw a serpent depicting a sinusoidal wave in Egypt's Valley of the Queens. In our human form, we work on our ever-evolving life project with constant ups and downs and ongoing interactions forming a pattern, like a sinewave. Science has shown us that everything is made of waves and all wave shapes are various arrangements of a single wave shape. This one important wave shape is called "the sinewave." Born human, we live in a dynamic environment, always going through ebbs and flows of circumstances. The waves shape and mold us into the unique individuals we came here to be.

The serpent in the shape of a sinusoidal wave in the painted tombs of the pharaohs, Valley of the Queens, Egypt

PROLOGUE

As quantum beings, everything within us is moving and changing from moment to moment. We breathe in and out, our muscles contract and expand, our thoughts become positive and negative, and our relationships go well sometimes and not so well. A dance is being played out in our life due to the binary nature of constant ebb and flow.

The best way to see this for yourself is by looking at a bird flying in the sky. There is a rhythm in the bird's movement while the bird is balancing against the wind. Do we love ourselves enough to choose to move our bodies in the rhythm that allows us to reach our highest potential?

I was born and raised as an orthodox Muslim in Karachi, Pakistan. The rhythm of my life started moving at a faster pace when I came to the United States in 1992, soon after an arranged marriage. I was only 21 upon my arrival in Los Angeles, CA. I couldn't speak English and didn't have any financial means. Being new to a country like the United States felt like being on a new planet and was complicated by the fact that I was accompanying a man I barely knew.

Life began to take me down a path filled with hard lessons, emotionally challenging experiences, roadblocks, and cultural and language barriers. But there were also detours, opportunities, wise quantum beings, and angels along that path. I chose to avail myself of all of them. When we intentionally avail our spark and will, we bring our quantum being existence to life. We bring forth the best versions of ourselves.

Today, I feel like I am living the adventurous life of a *Star Trek* cadet. My current career working for the National Aeronautics and Space Administration (NASA) allows me to be part of a team, making it possible for the first woman to walk on the Moon. If angels had come down from the sky and shown me a video of my future, my life today, I would have said, "This can't be me!" Never would I have imagined that one day as a rocket scientist, I would work on missiles, rockets, and satellites to enable humanity to live in outer space away from Earth.

How did I come this far despite my conservative upbringing?

How did I break through all the cultural, social, and religious barriers?

How did I stay strong through the storms and come far enough to touch the stars - to live in a world where science fiction is becoming a Reality?

How did I navigate my life to draw happiness and independence?

Living an expansive life as a dreamer and believer in dreams coming true has transformed my Reality drastically numerous times in my life when my threshold has been tested. Therefore, I have honed this art of changing Reality by availing the quantum principles. We are not a coincidence of nature in a carbon-based body. We are well-choreographed as a unique human craft. We are mighty quantum beings, and no one should be able to deny us our livelihood or our birthright. A human being can move a mountain if they carry a belief in their core and have the necessary drive. Being driven can propel you to be persistent; being persistent can make you consistent and being consistent can make you resilient. And so on. The key is to continue the quest of life no matter the hardship.

Quantum is the Latin word for amount. This means the most discrete unit of any physical property, such as energy or matter. Quantum effects can vary from an object 100 miles wide to the microscopic. Superconductors and superfluid's show quantum effects on a microscopic level. Once we understand how, human beings existing in the microcosm can affect the macrocosm.

You are here to understand how to create a quantum effect. We can make a minuscule change in our life, which can have a long-lasting recursive effect. The small can affect the large. One quantum being can affect the many other human beings they encounter. This understanding makes us very powerful and responsible for all our actions and reactions.

Quantum human beings are magnificent because:

> *We have everything we need inside us.*
> *We are leaders of tomorrow.*
> *We are the treasure, seeking itself to eternity.*
> *We are great manifestors.*
> *We are walking and talking miracles.*

My life journey has prepared me to receive and understand ancient secret information. I am embarking on this journey with you to shed light on how to consciously vibrate as a quantum being and unveil your soul's journey and purpose so you may live a magnificent life.

My hope is to positively affect humanity by sharing my story and raising awareness and understanding of our human craft and our power within. This book is for everyone who is looking to get a little push in life to move forward.

You must be open-minded and willing to step outside the box. The concepts mentioned here are based on years of self-learning via multiple Mystery School teachings. As a life coach and spiritual teacher, I welcome anyone who can be self-disciplined enough to comprehend these more profound concepts and self-transform their lives.

While reading, your transformation will begin and continue unfolding while you keep this book in your energy field. You can use the teachings in this book to reach your highest potential.

As "quantum beings," we are more remarkable than a space rocket; we can turn on our own ignition to launch our dream life. We have all the machinery inside of us required for optimum operation. When we understand our quantum nature of existence, then we can harness our innate power and create our dream life. This dream life is one in which we are best suited to reach our highest potential. We can affect others like a ripple in the water as we collectively co-create our universe.

> *As quantum beings, we are a conduit*
> *Between human and divine!*

"Quantum Beings," the guidebook to your dream life, bridges the gap between the two sides of the ladder. One above, another below. These two sides are comprised of physical and non-physical, spiritual and science, faith and fact, physics, and metaphysics. This book will help you see the truth for yourself by showing you the magnificent interconnectedness we have all around us and within us guiding our pathway to our true self, our home, and our final destiny.

In this book, I am giving you a recipe for a Magickal life. The sooner you implement this Magick in your daily life, the sooner you will navigate life with a state of peace and calm that comes with innate wisdom and knowledge. Living with quantum being understanding, we learn to embody our Magickal self in every moment we breathe, every image we visualize. Magick is the art of causing alchemy in our daily experiences. We experience Magick by living a dream life through our actions, becoming co-creators of the new and better world we desire.

Scan the code above with you smart phone to view a
message from Shehnaz – or follow this link:

https://youtu.be/KiosISk7dEM

I explain concepts based on my personal experiences and intuition that may have not been scientifically proven.

Therefore, I urge you to follow your intuition in deciphering what messages resonate with you in enhancing your life.

Flight One

Soul Recognition

Inner Fire

Be a Voice, Not an Echo.
-Albert Einstein

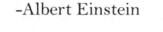

My age 1 childhood picture inside the apartment in Karachi, Pakistan

I arrived in this world during the fires of the Bangladesh Liberation War. Sirens were going off to warn the citizens of Pakistan to turn off all lights after sunset. This was done to maintain a blackout during the war. On the night of March 25, 1971, the Pakistani military pursued the systematic elimination of nationalist Bengali civilians, students, religious minorities, and armed personnel. My mother cradled me in her arms during a blackout in the darkness while a smile brightened my face. Right from birth, I chose to be happy despite my circumstances. An attitude of gratitude was embedded in my DNA. Happiness has been a trademark that has led me to people, places, and things that I would never have imagined.

Being a starry-eyed girl, I looked up every day to the sky in the bustling city of Karachi. I gazed at the stars and wondered about life. I dissected everything at the atomic level, down to the smallest fundamentals, to understand our existence and our reason for evolution.

My mind would wander in the multi-dimensional universe, asking questions like, "What are black holes? Where did we come from? Is there a life beyond the sky and the stars? I looked at everything with curiosity and questions. I asked about dew on flowers, why some people are poor, what I can do to help, why we have to go to the mosque, and why we have to give money to the religious leader who dictates every aspect of our lives. I felt similar to Sonny in the movie *I Robot*, who thinks differently than others.

Growing up in Pakistan, a third-world Islamic country, was quite an experience and proved essential for my foundational learning.

> *Our soul takes an evolutionary path best suited for us to gather skills and experiences for our next level of evolution.*

In Karachi, the typical household is extended and multigenerational, meaning you are raised by your parents, uncles, aunts, grandfathers, and grandmothers. My dad, the youngest son, lost his parents at the early age of 14, making our household more like the typical nuclear family in the United States.

My dad's childhood wasn't normal by any stretch of the imagination. When he turned 15, a bully splashed a colossal amount of sulfuric acid in his eyes. He could have been blinded. Instead, a powerful prescription for glasses sufficed. At age 17, he began carrying a camera everywhere he went and photographed the world from his perspective. He was brilliant at capturing life's beauty and its more profound message through his photography.

Due to his unique way of looking at and photographing life, National Geographic contacted him in 1969 with a life-changing offer. He had recently married my mom, who was raised in a sheltered environment, and already felt overwhelmed by the responsibilities of marriage. Therefore, my dad denied the National Geographic invitation and continued his business as a shopkeeper.

His regret at turning down this opportunity showed up in every aspect of our lives. Therefore, my image of my dad from my childhood was not pretty. He smoked, acted aloof, and was never content with the world. I saw firsthand what happens to a person when they are not placed in their chosen Reality.

> *By not making a choice, you are making a choice. Understanding this profound fact affected me throughout my life.*

The photo was taken by my father in Karachi, Pakistan. Picnic" 1960s.

A picture is worth a thousand words! My father took this photo titled "Picnic" in the early 1960s in Karachi, Pakistan. This photograph carries many profound messages. One of the messages is how everything tangible we possess is unnecessary when compared to the ocean's depths, soaking ourselves in the magnificence of Mother Earth.

> *When you don't have much to lose,*
> *you don't have much to fear.*

Fear is an incompetent teacher. We all need to embrace simplicity to enjoy life's sweet little blessings. Exhibiting courage, without the fear of losing worldly things, we can live freely and make life happen! What worldly belongings are you willing to strip away in order to truly enjoy the deepness of the sea?

My mom came from a very religious household. Despite being very intelligent, she didn't finish high school. She married young and didn't know much about life and the challenges she would face as the wife of a husband who could not fulfill his lifelong dreams. Being hardworking, my mom stayed busy with cooking, cleaning, other household duties, and raising three children.

I come from a patriarchal household, and my father dominated the family. The western term "he wore the pants" accurately describes the role he took. In a patriarchal culture, a boy is desired because the cultural belief is that the son takes care of the parents until they die. Sons mostly follow their father's footsteps by picking up the same occupations as their dad to keep the tradition going. Hence, my father would have wanted his firstborn to be a boy instead.

From day one, I was asked to fit in a box that didn't align with my true self. I was born and raised in a Dawoodi Bohra religion. The Dawoodi Bohras are a sect within the Ismaili branch of Shia Islam.

Being Muslim, we live by the five pillars of Islam. The five pillars are core beliefs and practices:

1. The belief that, "There is no god but God, and Muhammad is the Messenger of God" is central to Islam
2. Prayer five times a day
3. Fasting in the month of Ramadan
4. Performing Pilgrimage Hajj
5. Giving Zakat

Hajj is an Arabic word meaning "to intend a journey." The Hajj is the annual pilgrimage to Mecca that Muslims are expected to make at least once in their lifetime.

Zakat is a mandatory process for Muslims and is regarded as a form of worship. Zakat ensures that individuals who are helpless or lack basic necessities are protected from things such as hunger. The importance of paying Zakat reinforces the key idea that the wealth we are blessed with does not belong to us solely; it is a blessing from Allah that must be shared.

Being raised in a highly conservative religion, I had to go to school from 8 a.m. to 2 p.m. and then Madrasa from 3 p.m.

to 5 p.m. Madrasa is a school where we get religious training and learn life skills. After school, I would then be expected to do homework for two hours. Only after these duties were complete was I allowed to play, have dinner, and finally sleep.

Being the oldest, I was responsible for looking after my siblings when my parents wanted to go to the cinema. I was gifted with brains and talents. Being the brightest in school, I tutored my siblings. My siblings were not nearly as interested in school as I was, which I found frustrating, especially since my mother would blame me for their failing grades.

At the age of seven, I tap danced on a table, and competed in the school debates, and won. But I soon stopped being a multitalented person, as the Madrasa teachings started taking hold of my personality and interfering with my innate gifts. Per the conservative Bohra teaching, I was not supposed to dance, sing, or participate in any extracurricular activities. Instead, Madrasa teaching emphasizes a person must be controlled by their beliefs continually planted by religious training.

A girl growing up in Pakistan isn't encouraged to swim, play sports, or learn outdoor hobbies. Instead, we are shunned from anything and everything that allows us to understand ourselves fully. The only games I played, despite the religious dogma, were badminton and skating. I am very grateful to my dad, who encouraged my immense love for skating.

Growing up, I did not have a healthy childhood. I acquired many of the typical third-world diseases, creating innate resilience within me. Resilience is "the capacity to recover quickly from difficulties; toughness." You name a disease, and I had it, from smallpox to typhoid to measles and jaundice.

At the age of eight, I got very sick. We drove to a doctor who lived 45 minutes away from home. He came highly recommended for these types of serious cases. In third-world countries, bathrooms are not always available in doctor's offices. At the doctor's, I had to go to the bathroom badly due to diarrhea. Since I knew I couldn't hold it any longer, on the way home, my father stopped the car in a highly distressed neighborhood where people were incredibly poor. We explained the situation to them, and they let us use their bathroom. The bathroom had a hinged door with no lock, an uneven concrete floor, and a large hole in the ground. This is how thousands of people live in third-world countries due to poverty and illiteracy.

It is not my intention to paint a dark picture of my country, so I want to quickly highlight some unique and positive attributes. First, Pakistani people are very hospitable, loving, caring, hardworking, and emotional. Second, Pakistani culture is vibrant, full of colors, diversity, and unique art. Third, Pakistan is full of natural resources with breathtaking beauty all around the northern mountains of the Himalayas. But the culture is quite different from the U.S.

In addition to being sick, my self-esteem was affected regularly since my dad disapproved of my studies. Being pragmatic, he only saw my future as a good wife in the kitchen.

Generally, Pakistani girls only get an education to get a better husband and help their kids with their homework. I remember my dad saying to me, "You will die right there in that corner." The corner he referred to was where I would lay my pillow on the floor to make a desk and lean myself against the wall. There wasn't much furniture in the living room, so we often sat on the floor and ate there as well.

I didn't like having my dad around because of his ongoing depression and sadness. He would get mad at little things and casually call people names, including my mom. I challenged him with statements like, "Dad, since you are very well adapted in your intellects, why don't you apply that to your life? Actions speak louder than words." My instigation made him angry, and I was sometimes punished with candle burns. These candle burns didn't leave any scar. It just made me aware that I didn't want him to be mad at me because it would physically hurt me. The anticipation caused me more pain than the candle burn itself. Sometimes, I prayed for him to disappear from our lives so we could live happily ever after.

I have always been aware that I didn't belong here on Earth and that there is more to life beyond the stars. Even then, I knew that there was a world where drama and trauma didn't exist. At the age of 10, I wanted out of this dark and unfamiliar world. I knew that these feelings were very ill and needed to stop.

I blamed it all on my dad because he created a lot of disharmony in our daily lives. Because of this battle inside me, I took steps toward attempting to jump off the 3rd floor of a building. Of course, I analyzed all the consequences. I eventually persuaded myself against it by thinking about my mom, who loved me dearly.

My education has been a very determined act on my part. My inner fire burnt strong when I heard "no" to something I desired from the bottom of my heart. I missed many ceremonies and occasions just to be at the top of my class. I even tutored neighborhood kids, later teaching physics at the coaching center. As much as my father loathed my studying, his beliefs gave me more and more fuel for my studies. My perseverance paid off when I was selected as valedictorian in the 12th grade.

Choosing a profession for me didn't require a thought-provoking process. I have always had a drive, will, and desire to learn and continually grow. My parents were not even high school graduates; however, that did not stop me from pursuing further education. I initially wanted to go to medical school and become a doctor. My dad denied that proposal since one has to do night duties to be a medical student. In Karachi, Pakistan, it is not safe for a woman to commute at night. Rape and abduction were common then, too. My next choice was engineering since medicine and engineering were considered the two most desirable and respected professions in Pakistan.

Thankfully, I met the criteria for admission to the best engineering school in the country. Without my dad's knowledge, my mom signed all the admission paperwork. Deep down, I was fearful of my dad knowing about my actions. Regardless, I followed my heart without hesitation and received admittance to the prestigious Nadirshaw Eduljee Dinshaw University in Karachi,

Pakistan. This became a highly impactful, life-changing decision for me and opened doors to a life I could never have dreamed of as a young girl. It allowed me to be financially independent for the rest of my life.

I subsequently had an arranged marriage, a natural progression according to my lifestyle and religion. Arranged marriage was the only way one could marry in my culture during the early 1990s. In arranged marriages, two people are brought together by the supposedly wise elders of the family who have seen the world and know what can make a successful union. Generally, loving each other was never a criterion, so the focus was on family values, education, and wealth. This may have been because these elders never experienced true love themselves. In Pakistan, most couples stay married, so the divorce rate is low. Does this mean all of those relationships are happily everlasting? My parents had an arranged marriage. Their personalities, interests, religious beliefs, and ways of living life were drastically different. Despite all of this, they still stayed together until the end.

Even though my family was less conservative than other families, boys often approached me with love letters growing up. I never entertained any of them because I did not want to deal with the negative consequences. In my culture, if you fell in love, then your chances of survival were low due to honor killings. Honor killing means the murder of a woman or girl by male family members who claim that the victim has brought dishonor upon the family name.

I had just turned 21 and attended my best friend's wedding as a maid of honor. I wore a Sari for the first time. A Sari is a women's garment, or unstitched drape, from the Indian and Pakistani subcontinent, wrapped around the waist and draped over the shoulder. It varies in length from 4.5 to 9 meters (15 to 30 feet). This weeding led me to meet my future husband through mutual connections. He had just arrived in the U.S. and was searching for a wife.

Wearing my traditional bridal outfits for my arranged wedding

During my interview for the potential arranged marriage, my prospective husband asked me various questions. For example, "Do you know how to cook?" I said, "No, I can only make tea and rice." Another one, "Can you speak English?" I said, "No, I can tell you Newton's first, second, and third law of motion in English." (I knew this because science is the only subject taught in English at my Urdu-speaking school.) Despite my honesty, my first husband selected me. I was a high school valedictorian; therefore, he saw the potential in me.

My younger sister said, "I would have married him if this proposal had been for me." I overheard my parents the night before my engagement saying, "He is funny and offers a good character." I had received various marriage proposals from many men calling me intelligent and beautiful. Before choosing my first husband, my parents had selected a few highly educated men as prospective spouses, most of whom were 15 years older than me. I did not want a significant age difference, especially after living with my parent's volatile marriage, which included a significant age gap.

I agreed to marry my future husband because he showed attributes that were the opposite of my dad, such as being a workaholic. Making this decision brought me to America, the land of capitalism and opportunity. During my engagement, the only thing I could think about was an assignment for my Logic Design System Class. Having to spend the rest of my life with a stranger wasn't even on my radar.

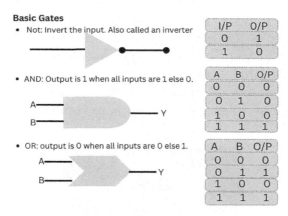

Basic Gates
- Not: Invert the input. Also called an inverter

I/P	O/P
0	1
1	0

- AND: Output is 1 when all inputs are 1 else 0.

A	B	O/P
0	0	0
0	1	0
1	0	0
1	1	1

- OR: output is 0 when all inputs are 0 else 1.

A	B	O/P
0	0	0
0	1	1
1	0	0
1	1	1

Logic Design System assignment occupied my
mind in the weeks before my wedding

A few days before my marriage, I received quite the shock. One of my married girlfriends told me that sex must happen on the wedding night for the groom to claim success in his manhood. I had taken advanced biology classes and still didn't correlate that human being mated the same way other mammals did. Due to my sheltered upbringing, I thought humans made babies because God knows everything. So, when a man and woman got together, God would know and decide to get the woman pregnant!

During my childhood, I had negative sexual experiences with male predators. I can think of times when I would be in the car with my family when we were out and about, and men would come and put their sex organs against my car window. It always made me very uncomfortable and resentful towards men. With these memories in mind, this information about sex on the first night of marriage led me to fall incredibly ill for over a week.

Isn't it an interesting dichotomy that, being in an orthodox and conservative culture, we are always kept away from men? Being away from men applies to all gatherings, both social and religious. Generally, sexuality is looked at as the biggest sin one could commit. But in this case, we get thrown into a marriage with a strange person with whom we are expected to have immediate sex on the wedding night. If this is not a cultural shock, then what is?

Speaking of my virginity, to date, we are still ritually mutilated, starting at the age of three. It is called Female Genital Mutilation (FGM) or Khatna in Arabic. According to the Dawoodi Bohra religion, this is a religious act in the name of "Taharat," meaning cleanliness. The practice is mostly carried out by traditional circumcisers appointed by religious communities.

A brief time of innocence before my basic human rights were trampled.

In my case, I was a seven-year-old girl. My mom asked me to go with my cousin to visit an aunt I didn't know. I remember being surprised because my mom had never sent me with my cousin to a stranger's house before. I went with my cousin and entered the filthy house. The aunty wore a traditional outfit, a blouse and a big skirt to hide her quite large body. She seemed to be in her 50s. She put me in a strange position as if I had a diaper she was going to change. I had no idea what was about to happen. She grabbed a blade and some old cloths and started walking toward me. She then performed the procedure without sanitization. I started screaming and looking desperately for my mom, who was nowhere to be found. I cried and cried. From that day on, I felt betrayed by my cousin and aunty. I bled for days and days and had to wear a diaper for a week. I was initially too ashamed to tell anyone about this experience.

Every single girl I knew, friend or family member, had gone through this torturous procedure. I didn't realize it was a violation of human rights until I came to the United States and met people who didn't go through it. FGM is recognized internationally as a violation of the human rights of girls and women. It reflects deep-rooted inequality between the sexes and constitutes an extreme form of discrimination. I have come to terms with this experience through my soul awakening and spiritual healing. We are all works in progress, and my healing continues.

Due to all these childhood experiences, my married life as a woman didn't start normally and had a huge learning curve. Only six days after being married to a stranger, I immigrated to the U.S. During my Rukhsati, a ceremony where a bride is given away, the bride usually cries as she is leaving her home, her parents, her siblings, her habits, her likes and dislikes, etc. She must embrace a whole new life she has no clue about.

As I was on a plane that was about to land, I looked out at well-lit downtown Los Angeles from the sky. I had never seen such an incredible city of lights with so much life compressed in it. At that moment, I realized I had left my hometown and come a long way away from my people, my friends, and my cherished childhood memories. I was very aware that my life was in for some big surprises.

No matter how misaligned our childhood circumstances, environment, or family we are born to, we also have an innate inner fire that is quantum in nature. This fire is best represented by claiming our sovereignty and right to continue to stand up for ourselves.

I survived because the fire inside me burned brighter than the fire around me," said Joshua Graham. As long as the inner fire is burning, we are continually moving into known unknown territory. This is the key to conscious evolution. So, let us continue on the path with our inner fire still burning in our hearts. This is how to live fully as a quantum being.

My tenacity not to accept "No" for an answer is the key to my success in making major life changes. My continuous persistence in following through despite obstacles is another key to walking a chosen path in life. I attracted a significant change in my life when leaving everything I knew as Real up until then. In my desire to create a dream life, I embarked on a journey that led me through many arduous challenges before this life could emerge.

Affirmation

I trust the quiet voice that emanates deep
within me down to the bones.
I allow this voice to rise to the surface
and take me forward in life.
I am loveable just the way I am with no cover,
no mask, and no makeup.

Keep Your Inner Fire Alive

1. What is your burning desire or the Song of your Heart deep within that allows you to sing through life?
2. What obstacles do you face in your day-to-day living that go against the Song in your Heart?
3. What is the one small step you can take today that aligns you with your heart's desire and helps you change your tomorrow?
4. Identify the help you need—people, tools, teachers, or maybe even a mentor.
5. Take one action today to receive the help you need.

Scan the code above with you smart phone to view a message from Shehnaz – or follow this link:

https://youtu.be/Rjtt0PCckXE

Chapter 2

Riding the Wave

"You can't stop the waves,
but you can learn to surf."
-Jon Kabat-Zinn

When I landed at LAX airport, my entire life turned upside down. I felt as if I had left Earth. I had never met anyone outside of my own race due to my limited travel experience. As I scanned the airport, I saw tall men, broad men, women of various races, and people of disparate weights and sizes, all wearing different types of clothing and having unique eye and hair colors. Seeing so many different kinds of people all at once made me feel like I was visiting a new planet — one where waves were crashing all around me.

This new season in my life required me to learn to surf. What is the secret to becoming a good surfer? The secret is those good surfers are carved over time out of perseverance and willingness.

Paddle, paddle, and paddle some more.

"Keep paddling" is one of the keys to becoming a good surfer. However, you need to find the rhythm that works for you and keep at it. You will find there is a time and a season for the rhythm to call you.

During my first long plane flight from Karachi to Los Angeles, I developed a canker sore, so we headed to Drug Emporium in Anaheim, CA, after we landed. I felt overwhelmed by the abundance of choices and direct access to many products. Back home in Pakistan, only merchants could access the store's goods, which were kept behind the counter.

When my husband spoke with the merchant, I realized I needed to learn to speak English because nobody here would understand any of the languages I already knew—Urdu, Gujarati, Hindi, and Arabic. Most of my education and familiarity were with Gujarati (my mother tongue from my mom migrating from Gujarat, India), Urdu (the national language of Pakistan), and Arabic (being a Muslim).

My fairy tale story came to a quick halt as my husband and I walked into our studio apartment in Fullerton, CA. I was astonished by the minuscule size of the studio. I paced back and forth and trembled, "Is this it? Not even a bed?" My husband responded with a hesitant, "Yes." I was raised in an eight-bedroom mansion in the upper-middle class in Karachi. My grandfather belonged to a very well-to-do family, so I inherited a bit of a lavish lifestyle. We were the first to afford the black-and-white television when it became available to the public in Karachi.

I needed to accept that this studio apartment was my home now, and this strange man was my husband; there was no escaping it. I kept my optimism intact and tried to make the studio my home, but I struggled immensely at first. I couldn't find places to fit all of my clothes. So, I overstuffed every drawer I could find.

To make things worse, I stumbled upon intimate pictures of my husband with a previous girlfriend. He told me he would have been married to her if it wasn't for his mother, who insisted he marry from the Bohra religion. Growing up in Pakistan, my understanding of love was "… a pure feeling shared between two souls who are made for each other for life." Discovering the details of my husband's prior love shattered my fairy-tale belief system. I was beginning to realize that it was just the start of my long journey through a very challenging life.

My second biggest shock came when I realized that my husband couldn't afford my plane ticket from Karachi to the U.S. Unfortunately, due to this being an arranged marriage, I was not provided much information about my husband, including his financial circumstances of being in significant debt. Thankfully, my dad kindly offered to buy me a ticket.

The first meal we had was three-week-old frozen Rice-a-Roni. Coming from a culture where we cook fresh meals every day, it was quite a challenge to swallow each bite of the Rice-a-Roni. I did not enjoy my first meal at all, so I quickly learned to cook after that. Growing up in Pakistan, every meal was fresh since we shopped every other day. It was our custom to go to the market, say "Hi" to the chicken we liked, and ask the butcher to give us the chicken that was smiling. Because we selected the chicken we wanted to eat, we knew what was going in our bodies. The vegetables at our markets were fresh looking and smelled wonderful. There was no concern about GMOs (Genetically Modified Organisms) in our food.

In 1992, there was no internet, computers, cell phones, etc.; therefore, I started writing letters to my mom requesting recipes. Writing letters was my only means of communication since we couldn't make an international phone call. The cost of $1 a minute was just something we couldn't afford.

One of my favorite recipes that my mom used to prepare for me is here for you to try:

Almond Chicken

Ingredients:

3 tablespoons olive oil or any healthy oil of your choosing
1 teaspoon chili spice
1 teaspoon green pepper paste
1 tablespoon ginger paste

1 tablespoon garlic paste,
Handful of fresh cilantro
1 teaspoon cumin seed
1 cup almond powder
Handful of fresh curry leaves
1 pound chicken
½ cup yogurt
½ cup tomato sauce

Recipe:

1: Sauté oil with chili spice, green pepper paste, ginger paste, garlic paste, fresh cilantro, cumin seed, almond powder, and fresh curry leaves.
2: Add chicken pieces, cubed.
3: Add yogurt.
4: Add tomato sauce.
5: Boil the mixture.
6: Cook for additional 15 minutes on low flame.
7: Serve with wheat paratha or rice.

Growing up in Pakistan, I was taught to imagine my husband as my lifetime lover, caregiver, and protector. My fairy-tale belief system began to shatter as I realized what type of life I had walked into. My fight or flight system had been activated. Being a warrior spirit, I knew I would find my way out of these circumstances, as I had found my way out of oppressive situations before. I turned to the Five Whys approach to solving problems I had used many times.

The Five Whys:

The Five Whys can go beyond just five. For example: if one says, "I am not feeling well." You ask, "Why?" The response is, "Because my stomach hurts." You ask, "Why?" The response is, "Because I ate a lot of food in the restaurant." You ask, "Why?"

The response is, "Because I was with friends and wanted to eat food to keep them company." You ask, "Why?" The response is, "I am a people pleaser." You ask, "Why?" The response is, "I look for validation outside of me." You just keep asking, "Why?" until you get to a practical and implementable solution. You are dissecting at the atomic level to figure out the root cause of the problem.

Financial freedom became my first and foremost concern. I was at a disadvantage because I couldn't speak English and didn't know American culture—how to dress and present yourself. I also didn't understand the difference between 5 cents and 10 cents. I eventually found a job due to my affiliation with the Bohra Muslim community. This job required me to be a merchant in a dry-cleaning shop. I earned a minimum wage of $5.25 per hour. While working, I made a sizable effort to learn about money and the English language.

I felt exploited by my strict boss because he asked me to do things outside my job description. He asked me to take out a massive, 50-pound trash can one day. Keep in mind I was a 90-lb. girl at the time. A tear trickled down my cheek, thinking of my time in Karachi. I never worried about getting my next meal. I remember when my mom would even bring me special almond milk, so I could do well in exams.

Mom's Special Saffron Almond Milk

Ingredients:

1 cup of milk of your choosing:
A finger full of strands of saffron:
¼ cup almonds, ground per desired texture
2 cardamoms, ground per desired texture

Recipe:

1: Boil milk with all the ingredients.
2: Serve cold or hot.

My job duty required me to open the shop daily at 7:00 a.m. sharp. I am punctual by nature and arrived by 6:55 a.m. every day, except for one. Our religion obligated us to do a particular prayer early in the morning for Eid-al-Fitr, an auspicious holiday on the Islamic lunar calendar. Eid-al-Fitr is a religious holiday celebrated by Muslims worldwide because it marks the end of the month-long dawn-to-sunset fasting of Ramadan. My boss belonged to the same mosque, community, and religion, yet didn't respect my religious obligation and still got mad at me for being late.

The job and the treatment brought me a lot of frustration. When I vocalized my dissatisfaction to my husband, he shared no emotional support whatsoever. I felt exploited by both my employer and husband but decided then that I would not accept my circumstances as my fate.

I started looking for another job outside the Islamic community. I sent out 200 resumes throughout Los Angeles and finally hit the jackpot with an interview. The company made global positioning systems (GPS) as a product. My interviewer recently came from Japan and respected Asians for their work ethic. My English was still a work in progress; however, my story of coming to the United States intrigued him. I passed the interview and landed my first reputable position as an associate engineer. I also doubled my salary!

The next step in my quest for financial independence was pursuing an engineering degree. During the preliminary meetings leading up to my arranged marriage, seven girls were lined up for the selection process. My husband chose me because I was a college valedictorian. Despite my outstanding credentials, getting accepted to an engineering school was an immense struggle. I applied at three universities, and my admission got denied at all three places. My transcripts indicated "Failed" for a Logic Design System and Technology class. This was a class I was not allowed to finish due to a school boycott that canceled my final exam.

The University of California, Irvine (UCI) is where I wanted to go for engineering due to its prestige. So, I used my problem-solving skills to speak to UCI Vice Chancellor Laurel Wilkening regarding admission. I looked her name up and made a phone call to create a meeting with her. I explained to the admission office that I had a unique situation that needed explaining to consider my admission. Even though I was still very concerned about my English skills, I did not let my worries take precedence over my ambitions.

I sat across from the vice chancellor and began telling my story:

> *"An arranged marriage brought me to the United States. I was enrolled in an engineering school, Nadirshaw Eduljee (NED) University in Karachi, Pakistan. I had to return to Pakistan to take my yearly exam right after my marriage to receive credit for the first year of engineering. Back home, the educational system is based on the 'all or nothing' approach, meaning that you get credit only if you take all your exams for the whole year.*
>
> *One of my engineering classes, Logic Design Systems and Technology (LDST), was boycotted when a rich, influential student who belonged to the school union became ill. The school union decided to boycott the exam. I decided to press on and take the test, even though the school was vacated due to the fear of getting shot by supporters of the boycott. One of the union guys approached me at my desk, put a gun to my temple, and said, 'Are you willing to die for this?' Of course, my life was more important than taking a test. I stopped writing. He tore the paper and sprinkled the pieces all around me. The feeling of helplessness overtook me as tears started streaming down my face. I still wanted to take the test, so I went to the principal's office and insisted on finding a safe place to take the test. The*

principal told me, 'You have no say as an individual, plus you are a woman.' This humiliation made me reconsider my loyalty to the country I was born into. It took one year for the test to be reissued for the boycotted class. I never made it back to Pakistan to take the test, hence, the failed grade on my transcript."

After hearing my story, Laurel not only gave me conditional admission to the University of California, Irvine, but she also pardoned my physics requirement when I challenged her to quiz my knowledge in physics. I saved myself two years of schooling by being courageous and vulnerable.

Speaking English is key to thriving in America. Growing up in Pakistan, English speaking was highly regarded in prestigious circles. I prayed in my Namaz (Islamic prayer done in an orderly fashion five times a day) to speak English fluently one day. To improve my English skills, I started speaking broken English with merchants, strangers, and my husband with no concern about how embarrassing it may have appeared. Los Angeles is an excellent place for an immigrant because people are very open-minded and accept cultural diversity. It took me approximately five years to speak English well. Language and culture are complexly intertwined.

During my engineering years at UCI, sometimes referred to as the University of Chinese Immigrants because of its sizeable Asian-American student population, I worked as a computer consultant to support my tuition. I remember when colleagues would greet me with "What's up?" I always looked up. It took me a while to understand that "What's up?" equated to "How are you?" However, I didn't understand the cultural nuances. When they asked, "How are you?" I started telling everyone exactly how I felt in detail. I soon learned nobody cared to know "How I was." "How are you?" was just a greeting in English, and the correct response was "Fine!" The Islamic greeting "As-Salam-u-Alaikum" ("Peace be unto you") was more straightforward. Of course, I went through many errors and embarrassments before I learned that lesson. The difference in language and culture was something I had to overcome. I learned to ride the wave by figuring out the peculiarities of American English.

Speaking of embarrassment, I once visited an arcade, played various games, and, thanks to beginner's luck, earned tons of tickets. I went to the shopkeeper, who gave out items in exchange for tickets. I asked for a "rubber," and he started flirting with me and invited me to the room inside. I was quite baffled and came rushing back to my husband. Later, I learned that "rubber" meant "condom" in American English—I thought I was asking for an eraser!

Within two and a half years of being in the U.S., I had completed an electrical engineering degree. I landed a great job working on the Inmarsat phone, a very expensive satellite phone, with one of the global leaders in the industry, Hughes Satellite Communications, based in El Segundo, California.

One of the proudest days of my life, graduating from UC Irvine with
a degree in electrical engineering. UCI Chancellor Laurel Wilkening is
pictured in her office where she made the fateful decision that changed my life

Looking back, getting admitted to UCI was a pivotal life event for me. I had to fight for the opportunity, which made me savor the victory even more. I did not realize at the time that this one moment where two women decided to buck the system together would lead to financial independence for the rest of my life.

Was it luck, or did my courage and determination bring me to a successful career as an aerospace engineer? The definition of luck is "success or failure apparently brought by chance rather than through one's actions." But, in Reality, luck is where opportunity coincides with preparation. I don't believe in coincidences. A coincidence is a remarkable concurrence of events or circumstances that have no apparent causal connection with one another. I believe it is no coincidence that you are reading this book.

There are only synchronicities, meaning the simultaneous occurrence of events that appear significantly related as a message from the universe across time and space.

> *Opportunity is just synchronicity in time, with synchronicity being the organizing principle.*

The time we have is time enough to do the task unless we are not aligned to the true path. When this organizing principle kicks into our awareness, we know what needs to be done and what doesn't. When we feel we don't have enough time, we might be trying to do more than we need to. We may not be following our passion which would automatically allow synchronicity to streamline the way time flows. Flow means to go from one place to another in a steady stream. Flow means we are in the zone and don't feel time passing since our feeling of oneness with everything around us makes our sense of time disappear.

Akemi G says, "Synchronicity happens when we align with the flow of the universe rather than insisting the universe flow our way."

The law of conservation of energy states that the amount of energy is neither created nor destroyed. This law is at play at all times since we live in a perpetual existence. If there is one thing that is constant in our lives, it is change. We can all agree with that statement. If change is inevitable, then the question is, "Why do we resist changes?" If you choose to sit in one place and people around you start moving, what happens? The change occurs even though you don't physically move. We might as well get with the program and make things happen.

We need to accept change as constant and not be startled by our daily changes. "Consciousness automatically chooses what it deems best from moment to moment," said Dr. David Hawkins. We are conscious beings, and therefore, we can create a new moment that is better than the passing one.

To ride the wave of constant changes in our lives, we have to adapt to our circumstances by molding our thoughts, beliefs, and actions for the desired outcome. We are given adaptability at the cellular level, emotional level, and mental level. We have the innate power to *choose* the wave we want to surf. We just need the willingness and perseverance to become a great surfer.

Be a great surfer!

While riding the waves of being human, we must learn how to adjust our footing as needed.

1. What wave is creating a struggle in your life right now?
2. What can you change so you can ride the wave more gracefully?
3. Is this the right wave for you?
4. If not, what wave would you prefer to ride on?
5. What is the main reason you are second-guessing?

Scan the code above with you smart phone to view
a message from Shehnaz – or follow this link:

https://youtu.be/Sl4mZbw4ogw

Chapter 3

Golden Cage

"Birds can't fly high if they are caged."

-Shehnaz Soni

S tars can't shine without the darkness. On day one, we come into the world, and the first act we perform is crying. We cry because that's the only way we can breathe. Is it possible that we cry because we realize we have been caged inside this limited vessel called the human body, like a genie in a bottle?

Birds are an excellent example for us to observe because we are familiar with seeing birds trapped in cages and birds flying free. Birds can use their wings and the air that moves around them to create lift. To enable flight, birds change the shape, direction, and movement of their wings. But, if they are trapped in a cage, they may expend all their energy and still remain stuck in place. A cage is a cage, no matter how beautiful it appears. So, what happens when we live in a golden cage every day? We are not allowing ourselves to take flight and soar into our potential.

What happens when we follow media and mass programming? We become spellbound and deluded into thinking we are lucky to be in that golden cage. Being spellbound is when a type of Magick controls your mind and keeps your mind "bound" or tied to something. Magick here means anything that traps you by creating an illusion to distract you from your path. For example, David Copperfield was a great magician. He would make you see the statue of liberty in the middle of Las Vegas.

Being spellbound is when your attention is caught by something, and you become transfixed by that spell, unable to look away. Our "spells" becomes our "beliefs" because we start believing what we frequently experience. Our beliefs create a perception we keep living over and over, like in the movie "Groundhog Day."

How many of you have been brought up with a fairy-tale mindset? In the fairy-tale Snow White, she escapes with the prince's help. Some of us hope for these fairy tales to become real life. In the real world, we have to break away ourselves. There is no savior outside of us.

While trying to adjust to life in the U.S., I hadn't paid attention to what I needed in a partner. What kind of partner is truly well-aligned with my life goals and aspirations? I was groomed to accept that my culture, religion, and tradition would lay out a plan for me without my input. So I decided that my fate had chosen him, and there was nothing I should do but accept him and embrace him with all my heart, soul, and body. I was enamored with him from the beginning because he spoke English, drove a car, and was tall, handsome, and well-educated.

Unfortunately, as the saying goes, "Monkey see, monkey do." As a child, I observed my parents' dynamic, with my dad being the dominant breadwinner while my mom was the submissive homemaker. I wanted to perfect that same homemaker role as my mother. Growing up, I was very obedient as a Muslim girl and did everything expected of me. I planned to be an obedient wife as well. I would say "Yes" to everything. Due to my compliant nature, for years, I ate cereal every morning that included a chopped-up banana. I don't like bananas. I wanted to be the best wife I could be. I dressed conservatively and attended social and religious gatherings in the mosque. My livelihood revolved around being a good wife. My obedience was out of fear of disappointing others and receiving their wrath when questioned or disobeyed.

> ## *I called my codependent relationship "Love"*

I liked being controlled since that was my experience since birth, and it was familiar to me. My religion, family, friends, school, and interactions were based on a control mindset.

As a child, whenever I asked a question at my religious school, I usually received a big "NO." This resulted in learning to keep my questions inside me. I was encouraged to accept everything without question. Instead, a storm began brewing internally with all these unresolved thoughts.

One major advantage of being controlled is not taking responsibility for your actions and blaming others for your unhappiness. We live in a society where victim mentality is encouraged. For example, we may say, "Well, I have no choice," or "I am diagnosed with this disease, and there is nothing anyone can do," or "I have PTSD, and therefore I am never going to be mentally healthy," etc. This mindset keeps us in controlled circumstances. We create a self-fulfilling prophecy by reinforcing behavior that feeds this type of mindset. It's a vicious cycle.

Growing up in the Bohra religion, my name became a big point of contention. My father named me "Shehnaz" because it was the name of the princess of Iran, Shahnaz Pahlavi. However, my dad misspelled my name, creating a unique name that I like very much. The Bohra religion didn't approve of my name, though, and suggested I change my name every time Syedna Mohammed Burhanuddin would visit the Madrasa and shake our hands. Syedna Mohammed Burhanuddin is treated like a God in the Bohra religion. He is the direct blood lineage from Hazrat Mohammed Mustafa, the last prophet who channeled Quran under Islam. My dad, being a bit of a rebel, told me not to worry and keep my name as is.

The rebel in my dad struggled to follow religious guidelines related to grooming his face. He was supposed to wear a beard without the mustache and let it grow indefinitely for the rest of his life. My dad didn't care to follow these restrictions and shaved as he pleased. However, I couldn't get married until he followed the guidelines. So, he wrote down 100 times on a piece of paper, "From now on, I will not shave my beard." He chose to do what was required so that I could carry on with my marriage. Immediately after the ceremony, however, he shaved his beard. He didn't care about the consequences.

> *I am grateful for my dad showing me that it was okay to break the rules—and also abide by the rules—in certain circumstances.*

The Bohra religion is predominantly run on the principle of power and control. The flow of energy is blocked regularly by words like "don't," "but," "you can't," "you are a woman and there-fore," etc. So how can we break free from this mental cage? I am inspired by Bob Marley's quote, *"Emancipate yourselves from mental slavery; none but ourselves can free our minds."*

We live in a world where our surroundings tell us how to live, think, and breathe, but your mind should be your only ruler. As civil rights activist Marcus Garvey once said, *"The man who can-not develop and use his mind is bound to be the slave of the other man who uses his mind."*

Let's fast forward to my life after being married for eight years. Life had become monotonous, and nothing was exciting. I felt like a machine following the same movements every day. I would wake up, get two boys ready, drop them off at daycare, and then go to a demanding corporate job as a software engineer. My successful education at UCI paid off in the form of a job working for Hughes Aircraft in El Segundo, CA, working on an innova-tive Inmarsat satellite phone technology. Later on, I got hired by Boeing Aerospace Corporation to support International Space Software (ISS) as a software engineer.

ISS was built in space via software to mate hardware with each other. Each piece was sent to mate with ISS via the commands and procedures followed by astronauts. This was our first time building a multi-nation construction project that also happens to be the largest single structure humans have ever put into space. Its main construction was completed between 1998 and 2011. The station continually evolves to include new missions and experiments since the ISS provides a platform for conducting scientific research, with all the necessary power, data, cooling, and crew available.

I would finish my day by picking up my boys, going home, and then spending the evening with my mother-in-law because my husband was always traveling for business. I put my babies in bed and would only get a breather for a short time before doing this all over again the next day. In the midst of all this, my mother-in-law reminded me of everything I was doing wrong as a mother.

My husband traveled 90 percent of the time, so his mom lived with me full-time. She was a traditional mother-in-law, and according to my culture, I was supposed to provide for her every need. She expected me to come from work and do my duty as a mother to my children and provide my undivided attention to them. If I would eat first because I am hungry before feeding my children, then it was considered wrong. If I would talk on the phone with my girlfriend, then it was considered wrong.

My role as a daughter-in-law started right when I walked into the house, and serving Shehnaz was never on the agenda. Based on the cultural expectation, the daughter-in-law takes care of the mother-in-law. However, working full-time and raising children with a missing husband is not the norm. Therefore, I did not support and provide for her as was expected, so she wasn't happy with me. Once in a while, we would get into an argument, and then she would call my husband. I would be asked to apologize to her since she is my elder. I felt like my spirit was compromised whenever I had to ask for forgiveness after a disagreement. It felt incredibly demeaning. My husband mainly visited on weekends due to his extensive travel. By the time the weekends would come, I was exhausted and despaired of any hope for a happy life.

Even though there was a great deal of commotion in my personal life, my work life shined. My bosses were pleased with my diligence and problem-solving attitude. I was respected at work, and there was never a conflict about what role I had to play. I just needed the same perspective to solve my personal life where my role-playing was dictated and controlled by others. I felt the crushing truth in this saying that played over and over in my mind: "If I was meant to be controlled, I would have come with a remote."

As a wife, I felt captive in all aspects of my life. I felt captive because my religion did not allow for thought-provoking questions to be answered. I felt captive because I was a mother of two young children—one newborn and one two-year-old boy with cerebral palsy. I felt captive as a wife because my husband traveled so frequently and only came to see me on some weekends. I felt captive as a daughter-in-law because my mother-in-law, who had diabetes, expected me to be her nurse, giving her daily injections. I had compassion for her condition, but she had no sympathy for me, not wanting to live the life of the perfect, traditional wife. I knew I wasn't happy. I also understood that I didn't know what was next. I didn't know how to go forward with my life and survive in the United States by myself, raising two demanding boys. I knew I could fly; I just couldn't imagine how my life would work outside of my Golden Cage.

As an engineer, though, I am a problem solver. I decided to "resuscitate" myself via "ICPR," a tool I created to tackle personal challenges when the situation feels hopeless. Engineers love acronyms. CPR happens to be the way we bring life to a dying person. I had to bring life to *me*, who was dying inside, through ICPR, which stands for:

I=Inquisitive,
C=Courage,
P=Perseverance, and
R=Resilience.

Being **I=Inquisitive** is about being eager for knowledge. I decided to interview everyone I knew who was married and had similar cultural values. I wanted to receive some outside input in hopes of becoming happier in my marriage. Also, being a people pleaser, I had to validate my happiness to ensure my perspective was not a fallacy. So, I started with my friends in the Bohra community. These friends shared their understanding of marriage and raising children, and their inherent beliefs were evident in the conversation. Based on their perspective, what I was going through was nothing out of the ordinary. "Suck it up, buttercup" was the ultimate message.

Being **P=Perseverant**, I continued my quest to figure out my miserable life. Perseverance required me "to continue in the course of action without regard to discouragement, opposition, or previous failure." I had recently started seeing a psychiatrist. The psychiatrist put me on Prozac, something traditional doctors frequently did in 1999.

I eventually decided to take advice from an unmarried friend outside of my community. She had a Ph.D. in psychology, and her suggestion was to get a divorce. She said, *"You don't need Prozac; you need a better life."* She hit the nail on the head, and it hurt. I discounted her opinion, thinking, *"What does she know or understand about commitment, responsibility, marriage, and motherhood?"*

Divorce was not an option for me. I was raised as a devoted Muslim girl, and as far as my ancestry goes, no one had ever done anything like divorce before. Plus, I didn't want to go to "hell" on Judgment Day. Isn't it ironic that we are willing to live in a hell in the present to avoid hell in the future that is placed in our minds by indoctrination?

> *My business travel became my escape from captivity and hopelessness.*

Working on the International Space Station (ISS) required me to travel to the NASA Johnson Space Center in Houston to test the boxes that interfaced with the Command-and-Control (C2) Computer. C2s are a "set of organizational and technical attributes and processes that employ human, physical, and information resources to solve problems and accomplish missions." I was an in-demand software engineer because I understood the ins and outs of all the Multiplexers and the Demultiplexer (MDM). In network transmission, both the multiplexer and demultiplexer are combinational circuits. A multiplexer selects an input from several inputs, which is then transmitted in the form of a single line. An alternative name for the multiplexer is MUX or a data selector. A Demultiplexer uses one input signal and generates many signals. So, it is known as a Demux or a data distributor.

During one of these trips, my colleague and I drove a rental car on highway 610. I started switching FM channels to find something I would like, and "Bingo!" I stumbled upon a country music song, "Where the Green Grass Grows" by Tim McGraw. My colleague smiled at my choice of music and suggested, "*I think you will like Houston because you like country songs.*" I would normally not listen to this type of music at home and noticed how much I enjoyed being away. I was a whole new person. I could truly see the grass being greener away from my "slave life." I could feel my freedom and liberty. The joy I felt on the inside could not help but emanate from the outside on this trip. Even my colleagues thought I looked happier.

At the time, we were living in Los Angeles, CA, in a small apartment with our family of five. Whenever I suggested moving to a bigger place, I was reminded that we could not afford a house. Generally, Bohra Muslims prefer buying a house using a loan without interest to follow Sharia law. Under Sharia law, interest is prohibited. Thus, a practicing Muslim can't utilize a conventional loan.

However, there was an alternative. My husband suggested we could relocate to Houston, where it was cheaper. So, we moved to Houston—the one rare instance where my personal desires did not conflict with being an obedient wife. My expertise, skills, and great work ethic with the Houston team inspired the leadership to offer me an upward career move shortly after arriving in Houston. I was promoted to lead hardware-software integration test engineer. I was now responsible for testing the software for all computers interfacing within the International Space Station (ISS) Program.

Working at NASA Kennedy Space Center, where I was ensuring the strain gauges and accelerometer were placed correctly

Working at NASA Johnson Space Center with mockups of the International Space Station in the background

After moving to Houston, my sadness increased since I had no social life. Our real estate agent, a tall, handsome Persian man, politely alluded to me many times that my husband and I didn't agree on anything. One day, he elaborated by saying my husband and I were day and night and finding a home to fulfill both of our desires was quite a challenge. My negative feelings about being a "slave" in my marriage increased with time. It resulted in me working late, and I would cry before heading home. I felt helpless. I had to keep moving on, though, so I continued my ICPR approach.

Not knowing many community friends, I asked my colleagues at work about their thoughts on marriage and divorce. They were surprised about my hesitation toward a divorce. One of my colleagues asked, *"You work, you take care of the kids, you do the groceries, you cook, and you are worried about being single? You are already living a single mother's life."*

One day, I asked my very sweet, happy-go-lucky office mate, *"What would you think if you heard someone tell you that I am divorced?"* He said he wouldn't care. He said he would think about it for a few seconds and then move on with his life. This experience made me realize how insignificant my divorce was to other people. My people-pleasing prevented me from taking ownership and self-responsibility for my own happiness because I prioritized others' perceptions of happiness over mine.

> *It is funny how when milk expires,*
> *we throw it away without even tasting it.*
> *When our soul contract expires though, we keep*
> *justifying how we can still make it work.*

I had signs everywhere saying, *"Shehnaz, your soul will die if you don't do something."* Signs are all around us to signal alignment—or misalignment —with our soul's path.

After much deliberation, I finally communicated my intention of divorcing to my husband:

> *"I am overwhelmed with all the responsibilities and feel like a married woman enslaved by my mother-in-law. I spend more time with your mom than with you. I feel like marriage has only given me the responsibility of three dependents without any of the partnership I was seeking from you."*

My husband thought I had lost my mind. He called my cousin, the one who was responsible for introducing us. My cousin and his wife, who lived in Austin, drove three and a half hours to visit Houston. They explained that I have a life with two kids and a family and that I can't throw that away just because I am overwhelmed and confused. They suggested I take naps every day upon returning from work to recharge myself, which was actually not a bad idea. They had some other great suggestions, but they didn't know the depth of the situation and how it was embedded in all aspects of my soul's survival.

In an attempt to keep our marriage intact, my husband asked my parents to visit us and put some sense into me. I had an army against me, trying to save my marriage (three parents, including my husband's mom). My parents made some observations on how I was treated day to day by my mother-in-law and my husband.

For instance, I always loved roses, but my husband never bought me any. One day, I bought a $4 rose plant home. I had a hectic life and forgot to water the rose plant. It withered, just like everything else was withering away. My husband was upset at my wasting $4, and his disdain for my feelings brought tears to my eyes.

My dad was a wise man and observed a lack of respect and love towards me. He realized that despite my equality in making the same salary as my husband, my mother-in-law treated me like a traditional daughter-in-law who should do all the house chores with my full-time job. How could I effectively do both?

In Pakistani culture, the wife stays home. She is expected to be submissive and cooperative with everything around her without personal wants or desires.

By this time, my parents had been living with me for three months. My father came around one day and stated, *"I won't be able to help you financially, emotionally, or physically; however, I will not stop you if you choose to seek a divorce."* Wow. I felt like I had won the lottery. Getting approval from my dad was the best gift I could have received. Now, if I dared, I could take my first step towards freedom.

I borrowed $100 from my best friend to make an appointment with a lawyer for my first consultation. Considering my husband kept track of every penny I spent, I couldn't charge my credit card for something like this. He would even complain if I spent an extra dollar on a loaf of bread. During my consultation, my lawyer suggested I open a separate bank account without telling my husband. Honesty is one of the main rules I have lived by; however, under the circumstances, I followed the lawyer's advice.

Being **R=Resilient** is the key to recovering quickly from difficulties and toughness. So, what kept me going? It was my belief that "There is light at the end of the tunnel." I believed life could be a fairy tale and have a "happily ever after." I just had to stay on my true path in order to get there.

Now, let's clarify one thing. I had been scared of the dark my whole life. I never wanted to sleep alone because I feared an invisible evil might get me.

Being **C=Courageous**, I decided not to let my fear of the dark hold me back from making this big decision in my life since fear can be seen as an acronym for "False Emotion Appearing Real." I knew that "courage is the quality shown by someone who decides to do something difficult or dangerous, even though they may be afraid." I remember friends offering to let me sleep at their homes. I responded, *"I have to overcome my fear and face it like a tiger."* When I started living alone, I would hear all sorts of sounds and get myself under the blanket to recite every Arabic prayer I knew by heart. In the "Tibetan Book of Living and

Dying," there is a saying, *"Your fears are the dragon that guards the gate to your deepest treasure."* This means where there is fear, an underlying treasure awaits our arrival. Therefore, we should conquer our fear to uncover the gifts hidden underneath.

My ICPR approach brought me to a place where I felt invincible and truly started seeing the light at the end of the tunnel. As I was peeking through the window to the backyard, where my oldest son was playing in the grass barefoot with no disruptions or nagging, this beautiful quote came to mind: *"Sometimes you don't realize the weight of something you have been carrying until you feel the weight of its release."*

At this point, my life had taken a jump start. I didn't care whether I would go to Hell or Heaven. I knew that I was very depressed with my life, and I had to follow my heart even if it caused me to travel to unknown territory. "When the pain of staying in an unfortunate situation gets unbearable, then the risk of unfamiliarity and exploring unknown territory doesn't look so bad."

You can go in and out of the Golden Cage if you choose to. The Golden Cage does not have to hold us in. We have the power to thrive just like birds have the power to fly. It can come with a price and trials for some of us; however, it doesn't have to be that way for everyone. The more you align with your true quantum nature, the more powerful you become and the more freedom you will experience.

The Victim to Victor

1. What beliefs are you holding onto that keep you feeling like the victim?
2. What choices are you not making because of your victim beliefs?
3. What beliefs can you create to make different choices this time?
4. Can you see yourself moving from codependent relationships to independent ones?

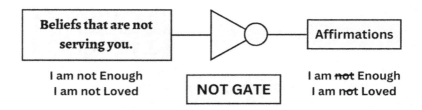

How do we turn our lives in a positive direction? Make a list of Beliefs that are not serving you. Pass it through the "Not Gate." The outcome is an affirmation you can use daily to reprogram your subconscious.

Reality Conversion Tool

This tool is an excellent resource to exit Reality and co-create a harmonized life, more aligned with your mind, body, and soul.

We all have all the power we need to save ourselves. The key is to first believe in yourself as the savior. Only you can save yourself. This is one of the hardest lessons we all have to learn, and one I claim only partial success with since it is an ongoing process. We just have to believe in it, and the path to freedom will flow from there.

What if I were to tell you that we have a built-in navigational system, a personal GPS that is designed to direct us to a fulfilling path? This path aligns with our soul purpose and is the most natural path to follow for our optimum life. To align with our unique path, we have to tune in to our personal GPS. We need to listen and trust that everything will work itself out. One of my favorite quotes is: *"Listen to your heart. The heart will lead you to the place where you will be free."*

You must have a desire and willingness to implement the solution once it is in front of you. You can't close your eyes and hope for the best.

Reality Conversion Chart

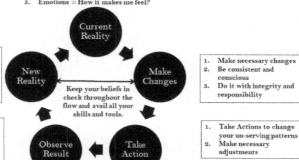

1. Challenge = Make a Problem Statement
2. Thoughts = Observe pros and cons
3. Emotions = How it makes me feel?

1. Confirm if "New Reality" feels good
2. What can I add to be more aligned?
3. What can I delete to be more aligned?

1. Make necessary changes
2. Be consistent and conscious
3. Do it with integrity and responsibility

Keep your beliefs in check throughout the flow and avail all your skills and tools.

1. Observe the results of your changes
2. Confirm the problem is resolved
3. Make necessary adjustments

1. Take Actions to change your un-serving patterns
2. Make necessary adjustments

This tool is an excellent resource to exit autonomous reality and co-create a harmonized life, more aligned with your mind, body, and soul via conscious action.

Scan the code above with you smart phone to view
a message from Shehnaz – or follow this link:
https://youtu.be/U19Aw3WJ-GQ

Chapter 4

Mobius Strip

*Exit the Mobius strip and take a quantum leap
to dive into unknown territory.*

-Shehnaz Soni

How many of you have been part of the rat race? Chasing a never-ending dangling carrot? Searching for an ideal persona of yourself? Searching for something externally. You go round and round on the same path, going nowhere, as you valiantly try to maintain appearances. It is like the head of a snake looking for its tail without realizing it is attached to the head. It only lacks understanding.

An ouroboros, a symbol in the shape of a snake that
represents the eternal cycle of destruction and rebirth

This circular symbol is called an uroboros. This symbol depicts a snake or dragon devouring its own tail, often used to represent the eternal cycle of destruction and rebirth. It is one of many symbols representing an infinite loop, commonly referred to as the Mobius strip. Sometimes, a Mobius strip is depicted with a person running endless loops on it, as if chasing after a dangling carrot that is always just out of reach. A dangling carrot is a popular analogy used in social media that involves exploiting an individual's vulnerabilities.

One example of this in our society is being addicted to social media. We are glued to our phones, like digital pacifiers. We are trained from day one "what to do and what not to do." We are groomed to become puppets and let others control us. This grooming actively persuades us to move away from our path and stay within a never-ending Mobius strip. *The Social Dilemma* is an eye-opening documentary that sheds light on how we are becoming like lab rats with gradual, slight, and imperceivable changes in our behavior and perception brought about by mass manipulation.

Mass manipulation causes imposed requirements to keep us trapped in the system. When you go to the Department of Motor Vehicles to get your learning permit, what is one of the necessary documents? A school enrollment form. To get admission to school, what is one of the necessary documents? An immunization form? Each requirement is a way of conditioning us to lose sight of how compromised our world has become. There is nestedness within each requirement to keep us hooked and enslaved. However, once you are aware of the Mobius strip, you are no longer in it.

When I came to the U.S. as an immigrant, I had just turned 21. I was filled with hopes, visions, and very high expectations of the American dream. Right after my first divorce, I felt spellbound and vulnerable. Like most people, from early childhood, I believed in fairy tales in which a knight in shining armor would come to save you. Have you ever been in a situation when you felt devastated and helpless and wanted a savior? There is a saying,

"Don't wait for the knight in shining armor. His armor is shiny because he has never been to war." This means we are so distracted by the shininess of an object that we don't see the missing piece. The missing piece is the problem we are trying to solve here. In my case, I was looking for a man who could help me manage my life with two boys, love me to the moon and back, and make my life feel effortless.

When we are distracted by shining armor, we don't realize that the rescue experience is not what we truly desire. What we desire is someone who can complement us and make us feel good about ourselves. In life, we are the only hero in our story; however, sometimes, it takes a while before we realize our own strength and power. In 2001, I believed my knight had shown up. A new man walked into my life. He was physically fit, good-looking, brilliant, sharp, and wore a thick, dark brown leather jacket. Initially, he showed a great deal of interest in me and supported me like a genuine friend.

But he also showed flaws, including being untrustworthy. We were in and out of our relationship as we processed each other's egos. During our breakups, he would move on with other prospects. And then he would want me to know about these prospects as if he was enjoying sweet revenge. It really affected me when I realized he was with other women since I was in love with him. Based on my cultural and religious upbringing, it was similar to betraying my love.

In 2003, he proposed to me on Valentine's Day. I didn't find it exciting because I had seen the side of him already that was not to be trusted. I asked my dad for advice, and he encouraged me to marry him by saying, *"If you would have one day to live, would you marry him?"* I thought about what he said and responded, *"Yes."* I would certainly marry him for one day. This fed my fairy tale belief and eagerness to return to normal family life, and I agreed to marry him. At that time, my boys were two and four years old.

Was this marriage a compromise or love? It was hard to tell.

I experienced both types of marriages. With an arranged marriage, you start with zero expectations because you don't know the person. With a love marriage, you have established expectations, which can have adverse impacts caused by disappointment.

We had a very dynamic marriage, challenging at times. Everything that attracted me to the marriage started fading away due to the newfound burden of responsibilities, lack of balance in partnership, and lack of appreciation. I would work all day long, come home, cook a meal, wash dishes, give my boys baths, and then read them bedtime stories. I became distant from my husband since he mostly occupied himself with role-playing video games. No appreciation was shown to me.

In 2007, when we moved to Huntsville, AL, I found a friend through the neighborhood book club. We would go on walks, and she came to know me as an independent-minded, strong woman. One day, we walked to my house, and I introduced her to my husband. During our next walk, she said, *"When I first saw your husband, I thought he was not a match for you. He must be an absolute sweetheart for you to marry him."* Then, she shared how furious she felt hearing him call me names. She suggested I pack my bags and leave him as soon as possible because he didn't deserve me. I told her she was overreacting. I was upset at my friend for giving me such an extreme suggestion.

> *After some thought and self-reflection, I realized that I had put myself in the Mobius strip of "happiness" for a so-called "normal life."*

No one else can define or create happiness for us. Therefore, when we follow the crowd in search of happiness, we get disappointed because we are following a shadow that is an illusion, a mirage, or "maya"—the Sanskrit word for illusion. I eventually became depressed from realizing I was following an illusion of happiness once again.

I needed to invest some time to truly find myself. Why do we say, "Find yourself?" Are we lost? Will we be happy once we find ourselves? What does it mean to find yourself? Maybe it means to embark on a journey, going down into the deepest part of ourselves.

Our soul growth occurs when we are in pain—physical or emotional pain. Pain hurts. Pain gets our attention. Pain teaches us a lesson we haven't learned yet. It's OK to take time to understand our pain, talk to it, and do what we think will help us work through our pain. Nurture your pain because no one else will. Avoiding pain will only prolong it. Exploring pain will ultimately be rewarding and help you "know thyself."

Just like any other day, I was shopping at the local grocery store. As I was leaving, I saw the free magazine "Natural Awakening." The title inspired me, and I wanted to know more. When I reached home, I started flipping pages and stumbled upon an advertisement for a class: "Metaphysics 101, taught Tuesday at 7 p.m."

As an engineer, I knew all about physics. But what is metaphysics? I looked it up on Google. "Metaphysics is the branch of philosophy that deals with the first principles of things, including abstract concepts such as being, knowing, substance, cause, identity, time, and space." My curiosity was piqued, and I wanted to know if this was something I should explore. There is a saying attributed to Buddha Siddhartha, *"When the student is ready, the teacher will appear."*

The Metaphysics 101 class was taught at night in the winter months. I was a little nervous about driving at night because, in Huntsville, there were few streetlights on most of the roads. I had night vision problems due to my eyesight being compromised by a past Lasik eye correction surgery. In order to attend the class, I also needed to ask my husband if he would be willing to watch the kids at night.

I decided to go check out the school where the class was taught, visiting it during daylight hours to establish some comfort around the idea.

As I entered the school, I saw mostly white women aged 60 and older. Everyone looked at me as if I were a new species they had never seen before. I felt very uncomfortable. I situated myself in a seat in the back, away from everyone. I started paying attention to their discussion; words like "telepathy" and "clairaudience" were used like ordinary words. Even though I had initially felt some discomfort, I felt then like I had found my new tribe. I felt oneness with everyone around me. Faye, an amazingly wise, older woman and well-known priest at the school, further confirmed my interest in taking the class. I signed up and immersed myself in everything the school could teach me.

Human beings are dynamic. Therefore, the dance between two people has to be renewed and revived to keep a marriage thriving. When two people are not dancing to the same rhythm, living together becomes troublesome. In June 2010, I prepared myself to consider separation and file for divorce. During that time, the Boeing Seattle company was working on a Program 787 Dreamliner plane. The 787 Dreamliner airplane offered fuel efficiency and range flexibility. The project was looking for engineering talent to overcome some last-minute challenges. My husband encouraged me to take up the temporary domestic relocation to Seattle for the program. My husband called this a "trial separation." It would allow us to live at two separate residences without paying additional expenses.

Within three weeks of working and being away from my boys, I decided to stop the trial separation and move forward with the divorce. However, fate had a different plan. While returning home, I realized I had missed my period. I bought a pregnancy test kit from Walmart, and my test came back positive. I couldn't believe it. I was overcome with shock and felt utterly lost. I took two more pregnancy tests, all positive. I asked God why he had done this to me and cried out loud for days. I finally came to accept my pregnancy after several days of torment. My husband was excited to become a father again and hoped this child would mend our relationship.

In Nov 2012, I took an "Access Consciousness" course, also called "Bars" training, to certify my personal growth. Access aims to create a world of consciousness and oneness. The course strives to get you to enhance your consciousness. I came home as a different person, loaded with rejuvenation and revival.

That day I entered my home, I felt extremely disappointed. I realized I had created a very chaotic life. My youngest, who was 20 months old, had filthy diapers soaked with poop. My boys were hungry, and the house was messy.

My intuitive husband, aware of my discontent and disappointment, blamed my patriarchal upbringing and childhood abuse for being the cause of the failed marriage.

"Our greatest fear should not be of failure, but of succeeding at things in life that don't really matter." This quote from Francis Chan highlights the fact that sometimes we chase something not entirely healthy for us or even satisfying. We pursue it because of the societal pressure of keeping up appearances.

Keep in mind that I was playing the victim and instigating him with my constant discontent. He was unhappy as well and came across to me as vindictive. Marriage is a dance between two people. I was not able to dance with him, so my disappointment created a vicious cycle that made the marriage unsuccessful.

My second husband was entirely different from my first. It was almost like the dramatic difference of going from 1st grade to 11th grade. He was a white man, extremely independent-minded, had experienced various relationships, was street smart, etc. Regardless of the differences, I still felt a lack of freedom in both relationships.

When I visited Pakistan for the first time in 10 years, I was cornered by friends and family who were eager to find out, *"What is the difference between a Muslim man and a white man?"* Being a trailblazer, I was the only woman in my family who had married a white man. My response to them was, *"They both have only one thing in common. They both are men."* The girls were disappointed with my response.

The end of 2012 was a revolutionary time for the Mayan calendar. A New Age interpretation marked December 21, 2012, as the start of a positive period during which Earth and its inhabitants would undergo a spiritual transformation. While the world was going through a birthing period, I was going through my own reflective period, trying to solve my marital problems. This pivotal point in my life provided me with an opportunity to continue on the Mobius strip without breaking my negative patterns.

My last attempt to save my marriage was in a letter I wrote to my husband in 2013. It was titled, "Dream Home, the Straw that Broke the Camel's Back."

Here it goes:

Darling,

Can you envision a house where there is Love, liveliness, peace, and harmony all around us? A happy home filled with love, laughter, and an environment for growth?

Respect should be given to the only female in the house, a wife and mother. An example of respect is not to call her names. An example of respect is not to humiliate her in front of the kids. She will also make an effort not to act like a victim.

We need at least one meal a day (mostly dinner on weekdays) where we all sit together and have family time. Not one parent cooking, cleaning and making sure our baby does not drop apple juice.

A husband and wife should sit together for a few minutes each day and give affection to each other without any digital devices around. Just quality time to build the relationship and go over any daily struggles, issues, or conversations.

Our recent trip to Melbourne, Australia, and staying with my friend has made me realize that it is possible to have some structured place in life when you are raising kids. They have a bedtime for kids, and then they sit and spend time together. The husband helps with housework as much as the wife does. Neither one of them said anything unpleasant about the other. This example of mutual respect is necessary for a happy home.

You believe that you know yourself do not need any help in with self-improvement. The only response I have to that is "that anger management" may be an area of interest to you. Also, we as a family need to have to work things out to communicate effectively with each other, which may require a few counselling sessions.

I love you, have cherished you, and want us to be a happy family. I do not like how our home operates and want to make it warmer, inviting, and loving for all of us. I realized that my interactions need work, and I must think before speaking. I am baffled about why you have been trying to send me away.

I like it when you show affection and love and want me to give you the same.

If you think you like this vision and want to help create this home for us, then we have hope as a couple and a family.

Please respond with your thoughts on this.

Respectfully,
Shehnaz Soni

I didn't get a response to this letter, and he tore the letter into pieces right in front of me when I asked for a reply. We went downhill from there.

I was repeating the same pattern with different humans that came into my life, just with new names and new bodies. I replicated an identical problem from my first marriage and established a Reality based on the beliefs I was carrying about men.

My belief that white men would allow me more freedom than brown men held me hostage. I realized that I could not attract the type of men I truly desired until I worked on myself by changing my beliefs. I knew I had to tap into my internal power, the same power I had used during my first divorce.

The source that I thought was feeding my soul was actually compromising it. The best course of action to eliminate what is compromising you is to cut off the supply. You need to recover from the damage and enable replenishment. Considering this, divorce seemed like the only solution to bring harmony to my life and my children's life. In August 2013, we separated. I filed for divorce in September of that year, and the divorce was finalized by December 23. I was left with four angry boys who didn't understand my reason for divorce.

In the process of chasing "a successful life" on a Mobius strip, I found myself with more significant challenges. I was out of the frying pan and into the fire. Was I chasing happiness or success? I was living in self-induced slavery and put myself in a bigger mess this time by following a dangling carrot. What is happiness anyway? Is my definition of happiness the same as yours? Not really.

Happiness is a sense of well-being, joy, or contentment. When people are successful, safe, or lucky, they feel happiness. Based on this definition, we should be responsible for our own state of joy, contentment, and well-being.

Why was I not feeling happy, despite achieving everything one could generally hope for? A quote that I love from Mark Twain is, *"Sing like no one's listening, love like you've never been hurt, dance like nobody's watching, and live like it's Heaven on Earth."* Of course, it is easier said than done. This quote is all about permitting yourself to be who you want to be with no judgment or labels. Therefore, the question you need to ask yourself is, what are you holding onto that results from external influences and perceptions?

To find happiness, we have to take full accountability for what happens to us. We are human beings, great manifesters, who can experience the Reality of our choosing by availing all our miraculous faculties. We celebrate Independence Day for our country to memorialize a historical moment. We need to celebrate independence for ourselves as well. Independence means freedom from outside control or support. This is a great time for us to reflect on life and celebrate our accomplishments in the name of independence.

We should always have the freedom to speak our truth, the freedom to follow our intuition, and the freedom to live our dream life. We have a birthright to embrace and exude freedom. *"Intuition is when you don't know how you know, but you know you know, and you know you knew, and that is all you need to know,"* as said by the character Zen to Zony. We just have to have faith that we can access our consciousness via our intuition. We must add wisdom to transcend our energies, like an alchemist.

Intuition is my inner gauge, my inner voice telling me to go visit a friend today whom I haven't seen in a while because they will provide me with growth and evolution. Intuition precedes logic. Intuition requires faith to take the next step without understanding the full picture of the outcome.

> ### *This is because intuition is the ability to know something without having proof.*

One thing that should be taught from birth is, "Follow your intuition." We should be using our full potential. Our souls can become aligned to our higher self, making us more useful to ourselves and others. Knowing yourself will reduce the chaos that is all around us. The book "Women Who Run with the Wolves" defines intuition:

> *"Intuition is the soul-voice speaking. Intuition senses the directions to go in for the most benefit. It is self-preserving, has a grasp of underlying motive and intentions, and chooses what will cause the least amount of fragmenting in the psyche."*

We need to continually remind ourselves of Imam Hazrat Ali's quote to ensure we don't contribute to participating in the problem.

> *"As leaders, we have to know what actions to take under every circumstance that presents itself. Aim to live in the world without allowing the world to live inside you because when a boat sits on the water, it sails perfectly, but when water enters inside the boat, it sinks."*

Hence, I decided to spend my waking hours in self-exploration to dream without anyone else's limiting beliefs. I decided to create a life free from mass media's definition of success. Exploring your dreams is a never-ending journey. It is never-ending because the more you dream, the more you learn about yourself; the more you learn about yourself, the more you realize you don't know about the world. Knowledge leads to more awareness of how much you know and don't know.

If we feel like it is *Groundhog Day* every day, with events continually repeating themselves, then we need to break free from enslavement. In the movie *Free Guy*, Artificial Intelligence, hidden in the form of intelligent consciousness, takes charge to create a very different Reality based on choosing to exit from the day-to-day routine designed by the coder. Break free from the Mobius strip! You are the creator. We are the creator. If we have the power to stay in the Mobius strip, we also have the power to exit the Mobius strip. We get to decide what we create as our next experience.

Exit the Mobius Strip

1. What might be a dangling carrot or mass brainwashing in your life? Which of those items should be eliminated from your life?
2. What is the worst thing that can happen if you eliminate the items from #1?
3. Can you live with yourself if that worst thing happens to you?
4. How would you spend your time once you have eliminated what is hindering you from moving forward?
5. Imagine your life now implementing #s 2 and 4.

Express it in writing via a journal or capture images via a vision board.

Scan the code above with you smart phone to view a message from Shehnaz – for follow this link:

https://youtu.be/h4j13burmZ8

Flight Two

Soul Awakening

Chapter 5

Being Human

Beingness is an art where we truly birth our future.

-Shehnaz Soni

We are called a "human being" for a reason. The name speaks for itself and suggests being in a state of "being," navigating life aware at all times of our existence. We exist in the physical dimension. We also exist in non-physical dimensions. We are a conglomeration of both the physical and the non-physical. We are spirits in the human body, not the other way around.

Therefore, integrating both physical and non-physical versions of ourselves is the key to existing and operating as quantum beings. The principle of correspondence represents the interaction between the macrocosm and the microcosm. It is through this principle that we are able to witness the seamless connection between the mental, physical, and spiritual planes of existence.

Nikola Tesla stated, *"The day science begins to study non-physical phenomena, it will make more progress in one decade than in all previous centuries of its existence."* Nikola Tesla invented the induction motor by harnessing alternating current, electricity, wireless communication, and binary coding, combined with other technologies, resulting in the ability to communicate through radios and cell phones. His invention has impacted virtually every human being on Earth and many in space. You, too, are capable of this quantum effect.

In our present moment, we are affecting everything that comes in contact with us at multidimensional levels because we are multidimensional beings. Multidimensional means we are layered beings, but the physical layer is the only layer we can perceive through our eyes. Other non-physical layers – emotional, mental, and spiritual layers are not visible. Eckhart Tolle emphasizes living in the present. Living in the present helps us to tap into ourselves as human beings and affect all our Realities in the past, present, and future. The more you make your present enriching, the more your life will be enriching.

We are continually experiencing the ebb and flow of life, and sometimes, we feel like the only thing we can control is our breath. Our breathing is the best gauge of our beingness and is the best way to show up in this world to manage our experiences wisely.

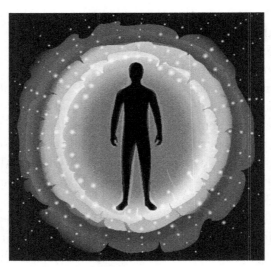

Artistic depiction of the radiating impact of one human being's aura
(This image is spectacular when viewed in color)

We need to be in a state of allowing. When we go through challenges in life, we do our best to ignore negative feelings and avoid processing our emotions. These challenging moments are when we truly need to be more attentive and integrative of our circumstances. Alex Collier states, *"The love that you are withholding is the pain you carry."* The challenges help us upgrade our quantum human existence as we process them with grace in a state of "quantum being."

> *Our subconscious reprogramming is at play, continuously feeding our future experiences.*

Most of the processing occurs in the hidden realm and follows the principle of fractality. Fractals depict a map of our ongoing Reality. The way we live our life through choices creates a map that is fractal in nature. This map of Reality is a good gauge for decision-making. Every decision we make ends up creating a pathway that is fractal in nature.

Let me help clarify this concept of fractality by taking a deeper dive into the patternicity we follow in our lives being quantum.

Fractal Nature is Self-similar

Go outside in nature and observe the trees and flowers around you. Lay down on the ground under a tree and look up at the branches. You will see the patterns in nature.

The light of the sun reflects off the water, creating a fractal pattern.

This pattern (in the picture above) is referred to as "fractal" and depicts the reflection of a reflection. This means infinite, complex patterns exist at small-scale and large-scale levels within the same natural object. This exhibition of similar patterns at increasingly smaller scales is called self-similarity, also known as expanding, or unfolding, symmetry.

These stunning fractal patterns can be found in art and nature.

Tree branches in nature express the Fibonacci sequence as
they split and form new branches.

Fractals are created by repeating a simple process over and
over in an ongoing feedback loop. The inner structure of a fractal
is reflected identically in its outer fabric. It is the same geometric
pattern repeated. That is why fractals are self-similar. The feature of "self-similarity" is easily understood through zooming
in on a digital image to uncover finer, previously invisible, new
structures. Fractal self-similarity means a nearly identical pattern reappears over and over.

Fractals can be explained by the following simple equation
called the Mandelbrot set:

$$Zn+1 = Zn^2 + C$$

The Mandelbrot set is a mathematical example of a complex
structure arising from the application of simple rules. What gets
created via this simple fractal equation is actually very complicated. We see nestedness and recursiveness with the creation of
an intricate emerging pattern.

We see fractality in all aspects of our lives.

To explain the two aspects, let's use a daily routine as an example:

1. You have a list of things to do, and your list says to call your doctor for a blood test. We number this task "1." When you call, they inform you that your white blood test count is high. Therefore, you have to retake the test. Now you have added another task to your list, "Retake the test." We numbered this task "2." You want to research this for your own understanding. We number this task "3." When you research, you find a connection to acidity in your body due to your PH levels and decide to drink high PH water to help make your body alkaline. We numbered this task "4." We keep making decisions based on prior decisions, and that is how we affect our Reality. We are participating in the fractal nature of our existence.

2. While performing a task, we tap into our beliefs, triggers, emotions, and past experiences and reveal ourselves layer by layer. There is a saying, *"Wherever you go, there you are."*

Fractals are also fractions. They can be scaled to any size, microscopic to large. The scale may change, but the ratio remains constant (equal to 1.6180339). This is a unique number and goes on to infinity without repeating itself. This ratio is called "phi" (not to be confused with "pi") and is also referred to as the golden ratio or golden mean. The mathematical proportions of phi are considered to be aesthetically pleasing.

Leonardo da Vinci, Plato, and Pythagoras have used phi to expand our sense of beauty, balance, and harmony to optimal effect. Leonardo da Vinci used the golden ratio in his painting "The Last Supper."

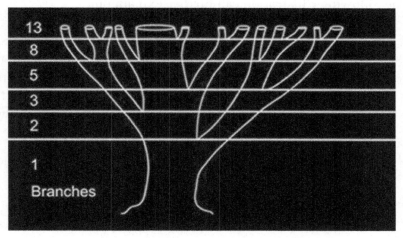

Tree branches in nature express the Fibonacci sequence
as they split and form new branches.

Sunflower seeds are a glorious example of the Fibonacci sequence.

The following illustration can further explain phi.

- So, in the beginning, there was nothing or (0).
- Then something (1) existed and decided it wanted to experience itself (1) relative to others for interactions (2), and later, a pattern emerged (0, 1, 1, 2, 3, 5, 8, 13, 21).
- From the first term, (0), the Fibonacci sequence grows through addition, where (0) represents nothingness.
- "(1)" represents everything.
- Zero plus (1) is equal to (1) and
- (1) plus (1) is equal to (2), and so on.
- By taking a number later in the sequence and dividing it by its predecessor, we can find a phi ratio of 1.618. Example: 144 / 89 = 1.618.

This number sequence, called the Fibonacci sequence, was rediscovered by the Italian mathematician Leonardo Fibonacci and represents fractality in nature.

The Fibonacci Sequence

1,1,2,3,5,8,13,21,34,55,89,144,233,377...

1+1=2	13+21=34
1+2=3	21+34=55
2+3=5	34+55=89
3+5=8	55+89=144
5+8=13	89+144=233
8+13=21	144+233=377

Fibonacci sequence math

What is a pattern showing that fractality is prevalent? Spirals!
I remember drawing spirals all over my school notes growing up. I also was very inquisitive about black holes at the same time. Barbara Marciniak refers to spirals as black holes.

The spiral pattern is evident throughout nature. I loved drawing spirals when I would put henna on a girl's hands during a marriage ceremony. In my culture, growing up, we would fill the bride's hands and other relatives with henna like a temporary tattoo as an act of celebration.

Henna art is used in celebrations, especially during wedding ceremonies

Our galaxy, tornadoes, sunflowers, snails, ocean waves, and pinecones all form from this first sequence. Everything around us is held together by particles from these mathematical ratios. A stunning example of the Fibonacci sequence is seen in the shape of a snail's shell. The beauty of fractality is created by an electron beam in an acrylic cube.

There are other various examples of fractal properties.

- There is natural phenomenon like electricity breaking down within solids, liquids, and gases. The branching form displayed by natural lightning has fractal characteristics, and these phenomena are referred to as Lichtenberg figures.

- We see our nerves inside our human bodies depicting fractal properties.
- Fractals are found in nature with the same atomic structure found in plants, animals, human beings, stars, and the universe.

Weaving the understanding of fractals, phi ratio, and the Fibonacci sequence makes us realize that the world we live in is filled with patternicity.

The ancient method of time telling is dependent on understanding these patterns of the cosmos. The measurement of time began with the invention of sundials in ancient Egypt sometime prior to 1500 B.C. The Great Pyramid of Giza has additional interesting characteristics, such as also being able to tell time. In the book "E=MC^2, the author, Pete Moore, explains how the ancient Greek philosopher, Thales of Miletus, discovered that at certain times of day, his shadow was the same length as his height, and the height of the pyramid was the same length as its shadow. This observation concludes that the ratio of the length of a shadow and the height of an object is the same for all objects if measured at the same time of day. Thales' unique way of perceiving is what made him a founding father of geometry.

A fractal world gets created via interaction and interference.

This is how our beingness determines where we will focus our attention and the type of world we create for ourselves.

Interaction

We live in an interactive world that creates fractal patterns based on our daily interactions.

Interference

Interference is the combination of two or more electro-magnetic waveforms to form a resultant wave in which the displacement is either reinforced or canceled. This means that the new waveform that gets created represents a dynamic between the two entities that interacted. Our daily interactions create an interference represented by Vesica Pisces. The Vesica Pisces symbol, commonly referred to as a Venn diagram in mathematics, explains relationship dynamics. Vesica Pisces is the physical representation of the interaction and interference.

Interaction is powerful enough to create another human being when there is a strong connection between a man and a woman in the physical form. When the man and woman come together via the art of lovemaking, a new human can be created. This new human comes from the vagina of a woman, shaped like Vesica Pisces. That is why the symbol is referred to as the womb of creation.

Vesica Pisces= Creation Symbol of union between masculine and feminine

Now that we understand the fractal patterns, it is essential to understand the effects over time since everything is in continuous flow. This is where bifurcation plays a role.

Bifurcation

At a crossroads, the choices we make determine our bifurcation. Bifurcation is the point or area at which something divides into two branches or parts. Bifurcation is the multiplication of the possibilities of Realities. It occurs in both continuous systems and discrete systems. Continuous systems go on and on forever to infinity, and discrete systems have a finite limit. In this context, continuous systems represent non-physical realms, and discrete systems represent physical realms.

When we eat our favorite dessert and feel the taste watering our mouth, the deep, dynamic feeling is driven by our consciousness. We have to be in a state of being to access this consciousness. This consciousness is the front seat driver. When we make changes due to a realization or awareness, our choices are different from our habitual day-to-day choices. This is how we perfect the bifurcation and bring more harmony into our life.

Bifurcation perfected is the golden mean and maps Mandelbrot's fractals. This means perfect harmony with perfect synchronicity. Bifurcation can be perfected if we master our decision-making process with the consequence in mind. Every decision will lead you to a certain point that branches. This point, where you seat your consciousness, will affect the Reality you will birth. It is similar to playing chess and knowing where your move takes you next. When no choice is made, it's like playing zugzwang in chess. You can say, "pass," and not make a move since all your actions have a poor outcome.

To sum it up, bifurcation is the fork in the road, and our decision affects our future and others. Every movement, action, and gesture have cosmic repercussions, either contributing to or destroying our inner harmony and the harmony of the cosmos. In physics, Newton's third law of motion, the law of action and reaction, proves it. Therefore, we have ontological responsibility for the well-being of the entire cosmos. In the movie *Cloud Atlas*, David Mitchell shares how delicately we are interconnected with each other: "*Our lives are not our own. We are bound to others, past and present, and by each crime and every kindness, we birth our future.*

Your path affects your destination and other's destination. Every
encounter is creating a new pathway of Reality in a factual universe.

> *The world is awaiting our next step and
> what we are here to unfold.*

For example, in my life, I have had to make tough decisions
involving children during my divorce. I knew that continuing
on my married path would lead to more disappointments in life.
These disappointments would turn into resentments and affect
everyone I love, including my children, the very people whom I
care for. I had to make those tough choices, which have impacted
how my children show up in the world today. It has affected the
choices my children are making about their future. This effect will
continue on to the next generation and the generation beyond.

When we play a video game, we only uncover paths if we
master the path we are on. A door opens up once you go through
a certain test and succeed. For example, in the "Dungeon and
Siege" game I played many years ago, my cursor would uncover
paths once I navigated a series of decisions. These paths would
light up as I discovered them. Our life is similar. We only get
certain choices if we position ourselves to make them available.

Otherwise, our paths will stay unlit, and we won't find those paths where treasure awaits.

Do you see how fractal our life is? How does fractality affect our Reality, our actions, our daily experiences, and our manifestations?

There are two aspects of fractals that are at play in our lives:

1. **Bifurcation:** A fractal pattern keeps branching off to a new state, like the branches on a tree. Thus creates a fork in the road, a crossroad. Our choice takes us to a different Reality each time.
2. **Self-similar:** When we zoom into fractals, we can see the part of the whole containing the whole, like a hologram.

Holographic Principles:

If you cut a hologram in half, each half contains whole views of the entire holographic image. Even the smallest moment contains eternity within it. What does that have to do with us? If each piece of a hologram has a different story, all those pieces need to come together to make a significant shift. What if this is the same concept that applies to humans? Each human has a part of the piece of the puzzle, and everyone has to work together to create a shift to make a significant difference.

The holographic method was unexpectedly invented by the Hungarian physicist Dennis Gabor in 1947 while researching how to improve electron microscopes. Hole means "whole," and gram means "message" in Greek. A hologram is a three-dimensional projection in a waveform created with a photographic recording of a light field due to diffraction (interference).

Pythagoras states, *"Everything is arranged according to numbers and mathematical shape."* The Great Pyramids, one of the Seven Wonders of the Ancient World, hold the codes to the truth through the language of mathematics. All the fundamental four universal constants are embedded in the architecture and geometry of the pyramids. Universal constants are numbers that are used for pattern identifications.

1. Pi encodes the size and spacing of patterns like a stripe on Zebra.
2. Phi/Fibonacci sequence represents a map of Reality and how fractal patterns get formed.
3. Royal Cubit connects 2D space to 3D and introduces a metric system of measurement.
4. Euler's number is the base for natural logarithms and helps with extrapolation.

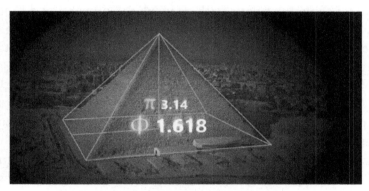

Fractal→Phi Ratio→Fibonacci Sequence

Patternistic World

Around the River Nile, the decimal system was used along with geometry to keep track of the fertile land after the flooding. Egyptians divided the seasons into flooding, germination, and harvest.

Flooding always occurred during the helical rising of the brightest star, Sirius, and lasted for 3 to 4 months. This is why the star Sirius is so sacred to the Egyptians. During flooding, Egyptians spent their time observing, measuring, and noting. As soon as the Nile returned to its bed, a big problem arose. Field limits would disappear. It was important to retrace the boundaries of the fields and start sowing as soon as possible. Also, the measurements had to be correct to avoid land disputes. Therefore, individual drops of water from the Nile River that didn't change over time were used for measurement. This fundamental discovery was made out of necessity thousands of years ago when harvesting after yearly flooding. The metric system, also known as the International System of Units, is used by virtually all countries in the world except the U.S.[i]

The bottom line is we live in a patternistic world as human beings. In living life, managing relationships, seeking approval, and fulfilling our destiny, we follow a pattern. Once you learn to recognize your pattern (for example, a sinusoidal pattern), then you can adjust your path as needed. You can get a hold of your life like a surfer who rides the waves, enjoying the experience with confidence and a smile on your face in a state of beingness.

We are each writing our life stories in a book with many chapters. We can say, for the sake of argument, that these chapters are a depiction of new patterns. What makes the pattern change? Triggers are the catalyst. What makes triggers noticeable? Your consciousness. Your awareness of your triggers and how much they influence your life experiences is a transformative process in itself. As you stay persistent with the process, you end and begin a new chapter.

I made drastic changes in my life, like getting a divorce for the first time, which went against my heritage, tradition, and comfort zones. Being foreign to the United States and not knowing my capacity to handle life with two small children was a massive undertaking. However, everyone doesn't have to make a major life change to trigger a pattern. You can trigger a pattern by doing something different, like eating out at a fancy restaurant by yourself. Based on the principle of fractals, your life will no longer be the same.

Cathy Davidson sums it up very well by saying, *"Learning is the constant disruption of an old pattern, a breakthrough that substitutes something new for something old."* Therefore, once in a while, we should recharge and rejuvenate ourselves by being alone and away from our daily patterns. Being a quantum being is how you tap into this awareness. This is how you can rewrite the script of your life and make necessary adjustments. The key is to see the forest versus the trees to make wise decisions.

I gave myself a gift and went away to the beautiful town of St. Augustine for a week. St. Augustine is one of the oldest cities in the U.S., surrounded by a wealth of artifacts originally passed on by Arabs, going back to Alhambra, Spain. The Alhambra Palace was built in the mid-thirteenth century under Muhammad ibn al Ahmar, Emir of Granada, to serve as the palace and fortress complex of the Moorish Nasrid dynasty. During my travels, I enjoyed small moments in life. I observed nature and natural laws that are constantly at play, soaking in the historical wisdom humans have gained through war and peace. I walked everywhere and refreshed myself with awe-inspiring experiences. I enjoyed sitting in a bar reading my favorite books on topics such as Tesla or ancient technology, all while making a few friends along the way.

My entire journey seemed choreographed by experiences led by signs, symbols, and numerology. Numerology is the spiritual method for comprehending and co-creating with the universe. Ram, a scientist depicted in the movie *The Man Who Knew Infinity*, was quoted as saying, *"An equation for me has no meaning unless it expresses a thought of God."* We consciously experience a universe that is governed by the laws of numerology; that is why math is a universal language discovered, not created.

Numerology is the ancient science of numbers, and math is the study of numbers, shapes, and their relationships. Each number symbolizes an energy force with distinct traits affecting your life. Tesla followed numerology in his day-to-day life and used it in his inventions to understand the nature and motion of the electromagnetic field.

> *I followed one step that led me to the next, and so on.*
> *It is good to be led and not lead. It is good to be*
> *in a state of beingness as a "quantum being."*

Be in a state of beingness! A tapestry is created based on your actions that maps your fractal world. Suppose we align ourselves with Earth and the cosmos and truly create a bifurcation in a way that creates a phi ratio, making a holographic matrix. Then we are able to create Magick.

Letting Go

1. Quantum being as a spirit: Remove the thought from your aura by acknowledging, thanking, and releasing it. You can burn the sage or palo santo. You can get life activation healing.

2. Quantum being as a mind: Remove the thought from your mind by acknowledging, thanking, and releasing it. Imagine the thought is attached to a balloon or a rocket moving away from your consciousness.

3. Quantum being as an emotional being: Remove the thought from your heart by acknowledging, thanking, and releasing it. Tell your inner child, "I am here," "I love you," and "I will stand by you."

4. Quantum being as a physical being: Remove the thought from your DNA by commanding it to be reprogrammed via affirmations. Channel your energy with an activity of your choosing – yoga, hiking, swimming, running.

Pattern-Changing Affirmation

I now bless and release all people, places and circumstances, and false beliefs which are not part of the divine pattern of my life. I now gratefully draw to me all people, places, circumstances, and true beliefs that are part of my life's divine pattern.

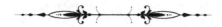

How to Change Your Pattern

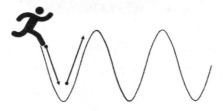

1. Identify your pattern
2. Identify your Position within the pattern
3. Adjust your Pattern if necessary via:
   >Disrupting the Pattern
   >Course Correction

Anyone can use this process to unfold unhealthy patterns to work through them.

Fractality in Life

1. Are you happy with the path you are on and where it is taking you?
2. What are you saying "Yes" and "No" daily?
3. What does your fractal universe look like as you proceed each day?

Scan the code above with you smart phone to view a message from Shehnaz – or follow this link:

https://youtu.be/3spbyVI0e0s

Chapter 6

Mirror, Mirror

Mirror, mirror on the wall,
Show me the mirror I am today.

-Shehnaz Soni

*W*e are the common denominator in all of our relationships. *"The people in our lives are mirror reflections of us."* This wise statement makes us ask why our experiences are reflected through the people and relationships in our life. There is an underlying pattern played out repeatedly with different people and places. It explains why we keep running into similar experiences even though the people and places have changed. It is hard to discern these patterns because the new relationships and new circumstances appear to be different.

We have mirrors all around us in the form of people, places, and experiences because, as the writer, Anais Nin once said, *"We don't see things as they are; we see things as we are."* We are channelers and projectors of Reality. We are experiencing a Reality based on our expectations, our past emotional triggers, and our beliefs.

The only way we can see ourselves is through reflection. The only way we can see God is through reflection. Reflections can be seen through a mirror, through other people, and through bodies of water. Water mirrors the world's vibration; you can see the reflection of the moon and sun in the water. The moon also reflects the light of the sun.

Reflection - Planetarium at Jaipur, India

We are created in the image of God, supported by both religion and spirituality. The Bible suggests in Genesis 1:27: "*So God created man in his own image, in the image of God he created him; male and female he created them.*" The book "Seth Speaks" expands on this, saying: "God is more than the sum of all the probable systems of Reality he has created, and yet he is within each one of these without exception. He is, therefore, within each man and woman. God can only be experienced through your own existence."

The world is a mirrored reflection of how we see ourselves. We are experiencing our consciousness through different aspects of ourselves like a prism reflecting light into seven colors.

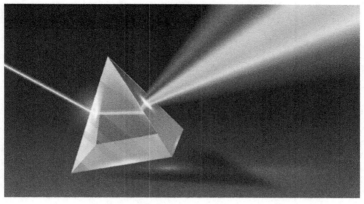

A prism reflecting white light into a rainbow of seven colors
just like we are reflecting God

We channel divine source energy through unique signatures as quantum beings, similar to a prism. This signature can be observed via an electromagnetic field meter that can measure the emitted electromagnetic field within a specific area. So, if the white light of the prism represents God, then the colors reflected off the prism represent humans. Each color has a special signature, just as each human is unique.

Sir Isaac Newton proved this concept of the coexistence of separation and union using crystals to separate light into the spectrum. He divided a wave into a particle stream in order to see the divided parts. He then used the crystal to put them back together. The result was pure white light. We understand now that, just like a prism, the different aspects we encounter in our daily lives are reflections of our whole life.

Everything we do daily is self-perpetuated based on the principle of fractality, where everything keeps unfolding like Russian dolls. Russian dolls are sets of hollow, wooden figures with the smaller dolls nesting within the larger dolls. As you remove each doll, starting with the largest one, a smaller doll is revealed within until you reach the smallest doll.

Russian Dolls depicting nestedness within each doll following
fractality principles

We must always look at our external circumstances to understand our current position. Keep in mind that external circumstances only show us one perspective. From time to time, my students ask me to teach them how one can change the world around
them. I always tell them: *"If we want to change the world, then we
need to change ourselves." Suppose you look in the mirror and see a
pimple on your face. To make that pimple disappear, will we change
the mirror, or will we work on changing our face?* When Gandhi
states, *"Be the change you want to see in the world,"* he is alluding to
changing the reflection in the mirror by changing our day-to-day
actions. If we are interested in making a difference in our world,
we must follow Gandhi's advice.

We see our reflection in the mirror every day and to fix
ourselves we have to go within

THE QUANTUM BEING

A documentary film called *Ethos* encourages viewers to engage in ethical consumerism and be mindful of where they spend their hard-earned money to enable the healthy changes they want to see in the world. These changes could be in our food, water, environment, and pharmaceutical industry. Being mindful of where we spend our money is the best way to make changes in our lives and others. This is also how we create a ripple effect.

Two types of ripple effects you may have heard of are the 100th monkey effect and the butterfly effect.

The 100th monkey effect derives from a study conducted in 1952, which followed the behavior of a hungry, young female monkey living in the wild on a Japanese island. One day she washed her dirt-encrusted potatoes in a stream before eating them since she was fed up with the residual taste of grit in her mouth after mealtimes. Her family watched her washing the potatoes with curiosity and then followed suit. Then her playmates copied this behavior, and their families followed suit. One-by-one, this cultural change spread throughout the community.

However, it was what happened next that was remarkable. This new idea went from being an exceptional idea copied out of curiosity to one that was the norm for all the monkeys. It was now a universally accepted and expected behavior in this monkey community. The researchers observed that the critical mass or "tipping point" for the behavior was 100 monkeys. After 100 monkeys had embraced the behavior, it became the societal norm.[ii]

The butterfly effect refers to a computational model of weather patterns in which the simple flapping of a butterfly's wings in the jungle of the Amazon (a minor event) can initiate a series of escalating events that eventually leads to a tornado (a major event) in Texas. The butterfly effect is driven by chaos theory. According to chaos theory, the butterfly effect is dependent on initial conditions in which a slight change in the state of a deterministic nonlinear system can make a massive impact in a later state.

Both the butterfly effect and the 100 monkeys effect remind us of the power of one: The power of one (ourselves), but also the power of one (one other person, place, or thing) to affect our lives in dramatic ways. Just like Russian dolls are layered one inside another, we build upon each other, one step at a time, one person at a time.

Once we understand that what we observe is only a reflection in the mirror, we can change ourselves and begin to live a conscious life. Philosophically, we are in a world of mirrors where everyone is holding a mirror to see a part of us. This appears to be external to us only because of our perception.

The universe is derived originally from the Latin word "universum," which means "all things, all people, the whole world." Please remember, you are the "u" in universe! The word "universe" can be broken down into "you" and "niverse," which is everything else. The universe is everything we can touch, feel, sense, or detect. It includes living things, planets, stars, galaxies, dust clouds, light, and even time.

We are the universe!

John Archibald Wheeler does a great job connecting the dilemma between the universe and man:

> *"No theory of physics that deals only with physics will ever explain physics. As we go on trying to understand the universe, we are at the same time trying to understand man. The universe does not exist 'out there,' independent of us. We are inescapably involved in bringing about that which appears to be happening. We are not only observers. We are participants. In some strange sense, this is a participatory universe."*

For Thanksgiving of 2020, I picked up my middle son, who was flying from Austin to meet me in Alabama. We had an insightful conversation, as usual. As we drove back, we discussed emotional control in response to triggers. Later that same evening, my friend shared an insightful post on Instagram, *"We are here to understand ourselves, not to be understood by others."* If that is the case, why are we constantly seeking approval from our teachers, friends, parents, spouses, and even strangers? Why do we like to be understood by others?

Why do we look for validation outside of ourselves?

In general, children's movies convey hidden messages that can help unfold our understanding of how Reality gets co-created by trying to prove we are worthy of love, acceptance, and validation. Most of us remember the fairy tale *Snow White*, where the evil queen says, *"Mirror, mirror, on the wall — who's the fairest of them all?"*

The mirror always replies: *"My queen, you are the fairest in the land."*

The queen is always pleased with that because the Magick mirror never lies. The mirror is how we see ourselves, and the Magick mirror enhances the power of the mirror.

But, when Snow White reaches the age of seven, and the queen asks her mirror again, it responds: *"My queen, you are the fairest here, so true. However, Snow White is a thousand times more lovely, fair, and beautiful than you."*

As the story unfolds, the evil queen goes after Snow White rather than processing her negative emotions and ego.

We all tend to identify ourselves with external labels. I use the labels aerospace engineer, rocket scientist, quantum healer, etc. Why? Because it makes us feel more special? Am I that special? If yes, to whom? Because it makes us feel more validated?

What is one thing we all have in common? We all have the same blood color. Bingo! Yet, we are all unique. Why? Because we all have unique fingerprints, unique electromagnetic energy signatures, unique life purposes, unique gifts, etc. Once we break free from illusory programming, we find ourselves and realize "me, myself, and I," all three of ourselves—reflecting back in the mirror. Every moment, we are pieces of a puzzle giving birth to a magnificent creation called life.

> ## *"We are here to transcend ourselves, not others.*

"We need each other to self-realize. Self-love is sparked by contrast. The more we drop into our own, the more we understand it's not personal. Because witnessing—true witnessing, it's awe-inspiring," - stated by my friend, Anouk Sophia, a woman of many talents who has traveled the world.

My artist friend, Carol Zukosky, also responded with some wonderful wisdom,

> *"It is within that we create, collaborate, and ride the wave of our experience of the multiverse. The fractals of our being, essence, are the reflection of life itself. It is an amazing gift that we can see ourselves from many vantage points. The hope for humanity is that we each reflect, integrate, grow, and make new choices, thereby adding to the collective dream in a beautiful, life-sustaining way. With a deep bow, realize we are deeply embedded in the mystery of life. I love you. My multiverse is woven with the field of light and love."*

To understand ourselves, we must understand our relationship with all aspects of ourselves and all ongoing interactions. The Seven Essene mirrors help enhance our understanding of all the possible ways people can mirror us in our daily lives. The Essenes were an ancient Jewish sect that flourished between the second century before the current era and the first-century current era. Seven Essene mirrors are perhaps most famous for their association with the Dead Sea Scrolls—a vast library of wisdom and information, untouched by time and cultural rampage.[iii]

Per Gregg Braden, *"The Essenes reminds us that we will go through each of these mirrors through this life. Sometimes multiple times and sometimes multiple mirrors at a time."*

Seven Essene Mirrors – Incredible insight into what we attract daily and why

1- First Essene Mirror

Reflects what we are radiating in the present moment.

Whether something is making us feel good or bad, in both cases, we are experiencing the emotion because of our inner dialogue tapping into our subconscious programming. It is related to our prior emotions and feelings, which generate similar experiences when we are triggered.

Our subconscious library is vast and based on all our experiences recorded in our DNA memory.

Ask yourself: *"Are your experiences showing you what you are in the moment?"*

For example, we wake up in the morning. We don't feel alert and awake but have to wake up to dial into an important meeting. When we turn on our computer, we realize that we are getting an unusual login failure and now we will miss the meeting. We feel concerned. We know that we are being challenged. This is an excellent time to go within and process our feelings before facing more challenges because we are tested through external interactions. That is why when our day starts with a challenge, it multiplies until we take back control. Our Reality mirrors what's happening inside us at that particular moment.

Gandhi elaborates on this phenomenon very well:

> *"We but mirror the world. All the tendencies present in the outer world are to be found in the world of our body. If we could change ourselves, the tendencies in the world would also change. As a man changes his own nature, so does the attitude of the world change towards him. This is the divine Mystery supreme. A wonderful thing it is and the source of our happiness. We need not wait to see what others do."*

Deepak Chopra elaborates, *"The Reality you experience is a mirror image of your expectations."* When you are having a bad day, haven't you noticed how everything falls apart? A vicious cycle is a good depiction of those bad days. Similarly, when we are having a good day, we feel the whole world is singing with us.

2- Second Essene Mirror

Reflects that which we judge at the moment.

Many people in our lives show us the same pattern of anger or fear; they may be showing us an inner truth about ourselves.

- Look at the people you hold most dear.
- Look at the qualities that push your buttons the most.
- Ask yourself: *"Are they showing me what I judge at the moment?"*

I have had the challenge and the joy of raising a boy who was born with cerebral palsy. He operates at a different speed. Everything that works for him is almost the opposite of how I operate. He brings everything I judge in people to the surface. His reasons for being different are valid, but still, my responses are the same. This mirror is very testing and tiring.

3- Third Essene Mirror

Reflects what we have lost in time and space and have yearned for as long as we can remember.

When we look into someone's eyes that we find attractive and feel that beautiful sensation, we are drawn to them, and something Magickal happens. We want to spend as much time as possible with that person. These Magickal encounters mirror something we have lost, abandoned, or had taken away from us. In the presence of this person, we feel an electric shock; our hairs are standing on end.

What is happening at that moment? Sometimes, when faced with people embodying the same things that we have lost in the past, our body expresses a physiological response that we understand as a magnetic attraction for that person.

Ask yourself, *"What does this person have that I have lost or abandoned or had taken away from me?"* You see what you desire through them. However, the feelings of euphoria generated in the presence of this 3rd mirror are feelings we can generate on our own. Anytime we give more credit to the person we are in love with than ourselves, we have abandoned ourselves. This mirror can bring a lot of pain when the person doesn't want to spend time with you or show that they care for you. It makes us feel all alone with our feelings and attraction towards them.

I have dealt with this 3rd mirror in the recent past. The person in this mirror never reciprocated my love or attraction. However, my ability to extrapolate the potential in people kept me hoping and waiting and living with an illusion. In this mirror, the work is done in the hidden realm of emotions and feelings. Only you know your suffering and heartache. This mirror was the most challenging one for me. It took years for me to realize that it was this 3rd mirror that was holding me back from the next step in my law of attraction.

The good thing about this mirror is that when the lesson is completed, the same person may come back for your attention and want to start over. It might be too late, though, because you have moved on emotionally and spiritually and may not feel the magnetism you once felt for them. If it is gone, it is because you found magnetism within yourself. It was always in you. Our perception made us think otherwise.

For example, I once fell in love with someone who wasn't available. After six years, he came back to me and wanted a relationship. By then, I was completely over him and had moved on with my life.

Just remember, we may think we have lost something. However, it is never lost. Our thoughts are tied to the belief that the outside world affects our inside world and gives us the perception of loss.

4- Fourth Essene Mirror

Reflects what we lose in the moment due to self-sabotage and destructive habits.

Throughout our lives, we often adopt certain patterns of behavior that become so important to us that we will rearrange the rest of our lives to accommodate them. In this situation, we find our behavior patterns may be compulsive or addictive. The 4th mirror allows us to see ourselves in the presence of addiction or compulsion.

It is interesting that this mirror is the 4th mirror, right after the heartbreak due to the 3rd mirror. We can easily become addicted to people reflected in the 3rd mirror and may go far enough to allow them to exploit us. So be aware. Because now we are actively messing up our own life due to self-sabotage.

Attachment stops the flow of life.

We usually don't realize it while we are going through it. For example, from time to time, I have been attached to a friend or new person whom I met and wanted to get to know and spend time with them. However, if they didn't feel the same, then it didn't happen. Due to attachment, I continued the pursuit. This behavior is addictive and very time-consuming. Through addiction and compulsion, we give ourselves away, little by little. When we give ourselves away, we have the opportunity to see ourselves more clearly as we lose the things we hold most dear.

5- Fifth Essene Mirror

Reflects our beliefs and expectations regarding what is sacred to us, namely the sacred masculine and the sacred feminine aspects of our Creator.

Through our relationship with our parents, we realize our most important beliefs and expectations about God, the Creator, or what is most important to us as our core principles. This mirror shows perhaps the single, most potent pattern that can affect us throughout our lives. It is the mirror that our parents showed us throughout our childhood.

As a parent, the life you wish for your children is the life you need to live yourself. However, most parents do the contrary, projecting their incomplete dreams on their children and sometimes living through them.

> *Children learn through you, more than from you.*
> *Your actions as a parent dictate your children's*
> *destiny more than your words.*

Through this mirror, we can see more and understand to a greater level why we've lived the lives we've lived.

> *This mirror shows us our operating system and*
> *highlights our fundamental beliefs and triggers.*

I believed in Heaven and Hell for the longest time due to this mirror. My belief was so deep that I was willing to live in a hell due to the fear of going to hell after death.

6- Sixth Essene Mirror

Reflects what we have kept hidden for a long time due to
our fear of feeling helpless and hurt, such as our
deep-rooted skeleton in the closet.

The 6th mirror shows us "the dark night of the soul"- crisis in the journey toward a union with God when we are ready to do the shadow work. Shadow work is working with our unconscious mind to uncover the parts of ourselves that we repress and hide.

Repressing our inner shadow obscures the light of knowing. Shadow work is where we find the fear, the jealousy, the judgment, and the negative ego. The shadow self is created by us as a safety mechanism. This is where the most growth and enlightenment can occur.

In January 2019, I got the opportunity of a lifetime to publicly speak at a UFO (unidentified flying objects) conference in Las Vegas, Nevada. I had my ticket, and my presentation was ready. I was so delighted and excited. The next day, I woke up with pain in my right ear. It was too much pain to speak at the conference. Unfortunately, I had to cancel. It kept getting worse over time and developed into a shingle in my eardrum over the following weeks. During that time, I went through a 911 emergency visit, was hospitalized, and then quarantined without any visits allowed from friends or family. Even after being released from the hospital, I continued to deal with trigeminal neuralgia pain and balance issues.

This experience affected me at the core level. Why did it have to happen right before I was about to follow my passion for public speaking? How could I get so sick that I couldn't even walk? I was given a message loud and clear about attachments and self-sabotage. My right ear was where the attack happened. I thought, *"What am I not listening to?"* The response came to me through my Kabbalistic understanding. Per Kabbalah, the right ear affirmation is, *"Filled with understanding of its perfect law, I am guided, moment by moment, along the path of liberation."*

When we attach ourselves to people, activities, and experiences while also giving them more credence than ourselves, we get our ass kicked because we are not on the path of liberation.

As we climb out of the abyss after losing everything we once held dear, we can see ourselves in a new way. This is where we find our highest level of mastery. This mirror is an opportunity to lose everything we've held dear in life. This mirror is where we let go of all judgment to see ourselves naked and vulnerable and accept who we truly are.

> *The 6th mirror enables optimum growth needed for our soul to thrive. The 6th mirror springboards us into the next higher level of learning and growth.*

7- Seventh Essene Mirror:

Reflects perfection in imperfection.

The seventh mirror asks us to see that each life experience is perfect regardless of the outcome, regardless of whether or not we achieve the lofty goals we may have imposed upon ourselves due to our perception of what we think others want from us.

> *We need to allow for perfection in the imperfections of life.*

We are continually invited to view our accomplishments in life without comparing them to any external reference. We can view ourselves with failures or successes when we measure our actions.

Being a single mother of four boys and working a demanding corporate job as an aerospace engineer, I took on a lot of roles in my life. I always worked on demanding projects with an aggressive schedule. I was doing it all while managing my household, my finances, the demands of raising boys, and still meeting my work deadlines. Due to being a perfectionist, I became very attached to having everything done right. This is where I ended up compromising my health.

Life is perfectly imperfect, and we need to accept that so we don't overwhelm ourselves and compromise our quantum human bodies.

It's best to integrate with our current circumstances to attract better situations in the future. Based on society's expectation of happiness, single, independent people may feel like they are missing out on marriage, partnership, and love. However, independent, single people exemplify mastery in the art of living since they don't have daily mirrors to process from a partnership. Being in a partnership is overrated. Sometimes, being single can be a gift since we can truly embrace the art of loving ourselves. Once you reach a place of mastery by yourself, you become available to attract a healthy partnership without any extra baggage. This enables you to be in a healthy relationship without any codependency.

To check on my progress as an evolutionary being, I have compared many other versions of myself throughout life. I see myself dreaming and manifesting all my heart's desires continuously by following one mantra. *"I can have it all as long as I live with integrity."* Why not? We are created in God's image; therefore, what we desire based on our unique mission is already ours.

I was led to be exactly where I am today through a well-choreographed plan. My becoming a rocket scientist and part of the team enabling the first woman to set foot on the moon only happened because I migrated to the U.S. via an arranged marriage. However, I had to take the leaps and risks to understand myself before I could be a proud engineer helping humanity. I had to stand up in my own power before I could symbolize power for others.

We are only aligning to our path so we can live in the flow. Being in the flow can make you more productive since flow follows focus. We can be in a continual state of quantum being. We can resonate with our reflection and navigate with more ease than before.

Alama Iqbal, a well-known and respected poet, says,

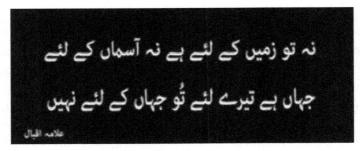

Translation:
**"You are neither for the Earth nor for the Heaven:
The world is for you, and not you for the world."**

Via reflection, we can understand ourselves. With this understanding, we can bring healing. Healing is revealing what is hidden from us through deep layers within layers. When peeling an onion, we reveal the delicate part underneath only after we go deeper into the peeling. We don't realize how deep we need to peel until we have peeled far enough to let the revealing continue without stopping for fear of getting hurt. This is how we hit the jackpot and truly make a transformative change.

We are invited to know ourselves in the presence of others through our relationships. There are two types of relationships:

1. Complementary: where there is balanced reciprocity.
2. Challenging: filled with lessons and sometimes toxicity.

Be aware of which relationship you are in and consider your options carefully to make wise and healthy choices. Remember, it is the underlying fear within you that keeps you in the second type of relationship. Your goal should be to attract relationships of the first type.

As those relationships are reconciled, we become the beneficiary of that healing. It is the benefits of this healing that we carry with us through life as we walk between the worlds of Heaven and Earth. Dr. Sue Morter quoted, *"We ultimately are made of Heaven, and we are on Earth. We are the gateway for those two realities to become one."* Ancient culture suggests, "Earth is a mirror of Heaven." Anne Wilson Schaef says it very well, *"What we forget is that we can have our feet on the ground and our head in the stars at the same time."* Let us bring Heaven on Earth together by processing all of our reflections wisely, one by one with love.

As above so below. Everything on Earth mirrors everything in the cosmos. Temples, mosques, and ancient wonders reflect the patterns and movements of the planets. An excerpt from "A Treatise on Cosmic Fire" says,

> *"A comprehension of this will be brought about if man realizes that all the planes of our solar system are but the seven sub-planes of the cosmic physical plane. It is the realization of this which will eventually unite science and religion, for what the scientist calls energy, the religious man calls God, and yet the two are one, being but the manifested purpose, in physical matter, of a great extra-systemic Identity."*

My working in space and living on Earth simultaneously allows a convergence of these worlds that will result in fruits that everyone can experience and enjoy. All these paths lead to evolution. Even when we think we are lost. We are only exploring the branch in our fractal Reality to find our true selves.

We can integrate all of our triggers to make positive changes by showing up in the world in the best possible way. The universe is only a projection of you. This is the key to your evolution. If you don't like what you see in the mirror in the form of people and experiences, then change yourselves. We are enhancing each other souls when we are with a reflection that is perfectly aligned with us.

Relationship Mirrors

1. Name and list all the relationships with individuals that you interact with regularly.
2. Assign each of the relationships to one of the seven Essene mirrors.
3. Which one of the relationships is the most challenging?
4. Pontificate why this is challenging for you in your life right now.
5. What are you not integrating that needs to be addressed?
6. Can you imagine yourself as a whole person without any of these challenging reflections?

Self-reflection Exercise

❖   What if, for a day, you replace your "I should" with "I want"?
❖   See what happens to your vibration and your experiences.
❖   Observe what activities you say "Yes" to and what you say "No" to.
❖   When you start living day to day with this unique vibration, your new Reality will unfold into a whole new life filled with new experiences.

Scan the code above with you smart phone to view
a message from Shehnaz – or follow this link:

https://youtu.be/umOY6VPaB2Y

Chapter 7

Weaver Within

The mind is the "Weaver" that carries the message in the form of an energy wave.

-Shehnaz Soni

*B*ased on the fractality in nature and the reflection we see through others, we are connected via some sort of invisible thread. Even though we might not be prepared to understand everything around us for its miraculous presence and the beauty that lies in the interconnectedness of all things. Interconnectedness is how we integrate our fractal existence as part of a whole. In this beautiful dance of life, we continually merge to strengthen our bond with each other and ourselves.

In school, we are taught subjects like math, biology, chemistry, and physics. We have a specific capacity to learn, understand, and make sense of things. This capacity lies within us. How can we understand this capacity weaving within?

The Weaver within is the song we can sing when no one is watching. The Weaver within is similar to the string in the guitar that creates a certain resonant frequency when touched by the musician. We have the strings within us that are our unique musical tone. This string is what makes us move in a specific way when we dance or listen to music. We lean towards what we want and move away from what we don't want.

The Weaver within can be utilized in our daily lives through kinesiology. Kinesiology studies the science of human movement. Muscle testing, also known as applied kinesiology, can be an excellent way to determine what is good for you and what is not. Neuroplasticity is also a fundamental scientific principle used in kinesiology to describe how movement and changes in the brain are related. Neuroplasticity refers to the brain's ability to adapt and change in response to experiences and stimuli. For me, I have an inner knowledge that is very strong and directs me to what I need to experience.

Energy exists all around us in all forms. To be human is to be in a state of vibration. As quantum beings, we are weaving ourselves using all the energies in and around us, including the thoughts we think that affect our vibration, frequency, and experiences. We can't see the energy; however, we can feel it.

Energy – Frequency & Vibration

Everything that exists (physical or nonphysical) is broken down into its simplest and most basic form as energy.

Energy comes in many forms:

1. Kinetic energy: represented by the energy of a moving object
2. Potential energy: represented by the energy stored by an object's position in a force field (gravitational, electric, or magnetic)
3. Elastic energy: represented by stretching solid objects
4. Chemical energy: represented by release when a fuel burns
5. Thermal energy: represented by an object's temperature
6. Radiant energy: represented by light, for example, "You look so radiant!"

For example: When we rub our hands together, we create heat energy. Potential energy transforms into heat energy.

The energy emitted and radiated around us can be absorbed or received by biological matter like the human body. That is why Nikola Tesla stated, *"If you want to find the secrets of the universe, think in terms of energy, frequency, and vibration."* Energy consists of a rate of vibration, oscillation, and frequency.

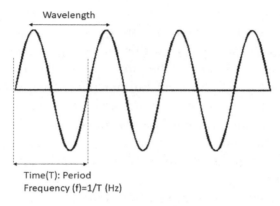

What is frequency versus wavelength?

> Vibration, also referenced as mechanical oscillation, is the change over a period of time.
> Oscillation is back and forth motion at a regular speed.
> Frequency (f) is the number of waves per unit of Time (T);
> The unit for frequency is a Hertz (Hz: 1/second).
> A wavelength is a length traveled during a vibration period.

Our words vibrate and give life. Based on the *Book of Genesis*, creation started with a word, "God," and a sound.

> *Sounds are created by vibration and words are created by frequency.*

Everything that exists vibrates, from an electron within an atom to an entire planet like Earth. Everything we see, hear, smell, touch, or taste vibrates. Consciousness is sentience, a person's ability to experience and feel. Consciousness is vibrational frequency. Albert Einstein says, *"Everything that exists vibrates in the form of energy."*

Whether this is matter (the things we perceive) or non-matter (the things we don't perceive), it is all energy." The great Albert Einstein demonstrated this with his most famous equation, the theory of relativity, $E=MC^2$ (Energy = mass multiplied by the speed of light squared). What this formula proves is that matter and energy are two sides of the same coin. Matter follows energy.

Crystals vibrate at a beautiful harmonic frequency and have healing properties. We can use crystals for healing because we are full of crystals. There is a resonance we feel with certain crystals because our vibration matches. The best way to know what crystal is good for you is by touching it, intuiting it, and working with it.

The subject of vibration is the foundation of a branch of science known as quantum physics. Even our thoughts vibrate. Every time we think, we broadcast our thoughts via brain waves. We are broadcasters and affect each other's energy at all times.

> *Our feelings (emotions) are a greater gauge than our minds (words).*

We, as human processing units, act like transmitters, receiving and broadcasting our signals in every moment of our existence based on our frequency and vibration. Experiences result from our thoughts, emotions, beliefs, and reactions. Our vibration and frequency affect our experiences, not the other way round.

We can be guided by energy. When we buy into other people's opinions, we are misleading ourselves via someone else's spell. That is why it is crucial to surround yourself with people who respect your boundaries. If we could see waveforms, we would know when we are emotionally compromised by people who thrive on other people's energy. The movie *Celestine Prophecy* does a great job of expanding on this subject.

Some people have trained themselves to tune in and out at will. For example, my ex-husband would sometimes pretend to listen. He would tune me out at will. One time I wanted to test my theory and said something nonsensical just to see whether he was listening. I threw the word "suicide" in the middle of the conversation with no context. He didn't even blink. His body language stayed the same, which proved my theory.

Vibration is actually what distinguishes one thing from another. For instance, the difference between the spirit body (also called the astral body) and the physical body essentially has to do with vibration. Although all things vibrate, they do not do so at the same speed. Some things vibrate much slower, and other things vibrate much faster. Things that vibrate slowly are what appear to us as solids. Things that vibrate faster appear to us as either liquids or gases. Everything from liquid to solid vibrates at an atomic level.

> *Everything in the periodic table is depicted as a different element, only because of the change in rate of vibrations.*

Why are things the way they are?
Why do they each have a unique signature?
Why are sounds different?
Why are colors distinguishable?
Why is something shaped the way it is?
Why are some people good-looking and others not so much?

Once again, it all boils down to vibration.

In the book "Once Upon a Time at Calvary," Benson Saili writes:

> *"The physical realm has its own frequency, which is different from that of the astral realm. To exist in this physical dimension, we need a body that is suited to it, that is, a body that resonates to or is tuned to the physical dimension with higher density. However, the dense body cannot dwell in the astral plane because its frequency does not resonate with the astral plane. Since it vibrates at a lower frequency, the physical body would be too heavy for the astral plane and would simply fall through."*

The physical body is denser in matter and has a different frequency and vibration than the non-physical aspect of ourselves. When we travel to other dimensions like astral, we leave our body behind and travel via consciousness. This experience is referred to as astral travel or an out-of-body experience.

What is the key driver affecting our vibrations and our vantage points? The principle of mentalism states that for anything to be, a thought must precede it. The book "The Untethered Soul" by Michael Singer highlights the voice inside our head that talks continuously, nonstop, and tells us how to run our life. Some refer to this voice as a monkey mind. In simple language, this voice is our thoughts. We must learn to navigate this voice in our heads through subconscious reprogramming. Because thoughts do become things.

Thoughts Become Things

We may not scientifically understand how our thoughts create our physical world, atom by atom. The book "An Adventure Guide to the Jungle of Time and Space" by Mike Dooley states that MATTER = Manifest Any Thought That Existed into Reality. However, I have also proved from time to time through manifesting that thoughts do become things based on the principle of fractality.

Thought particles travel along thought waves within our minds. Based on where we land in our thought form, we tap into the stream of Akashic fields around us and access the data stream. The Akashic record is a compendium of all events, actions, thoughts, and feelings that have occurred throughout time. "Akasha" is a Sanskrit word and means primary substance. Therefore, all things are formed from Akasha. Thought directs energy when we perform an action. Actions influence our experiences.

Every thought has its own frequency. Thoughts of love have their own frequency, just like thoughts of malice have their own frequency. Positive thoughts vibrate at a higher frequency than negative thoughts. We must recognize the deeper issues rooted in our childhood, especially when the voice is negative. Don't use your head; your heart monitors your vibrations.

Dr. David Hawkins derived a "Map of Consciousness" with a logarithmic scale to calibrate the relative power of the energy of different attitudes, thoughts, feelings, situations, and relationships.[iv]

The Map of Consciousness			
Name of Level	Energetic Frequency	Associated Emotional State	View of Life
Enlightenment	700-1000	Ineffable	Is
Peace	600	Bliss	Perfect
Joy	540	Serenity	Complete
Love	500	Reverence	Benign
Reason	400	Understanding	Meaningful
Acceptance	350	Forgiveness	Harmonious
Willingness	310	Optimism	Hopeful
Neutrality	250	Trust	Satisfactory
Courage	200	Affirmation	Feasible
Pride	175	Scorn	Demanding
Anger	150	Hate	Antagonistic
Desire	125	Craving	Disappointing
Fear	100	Anxiety	Frightening
Grief	75	Regret	Tragic
Apathy	50	Despair	Hopeless
Guilt	30	Blame	Evil
Shame	20	Humiliation	Miserable
The map of consciousness is based on a logarithmic scale that spans from 0 to 1000.			

Isn't it interesting that on Dr. David Hawkins's Map of Consciousness table, desire is a lower frequency, even lower than anger? Desire can put us in a desperate state of wanting something we lack. This is because what we desire becomes more important than what we have at that moment.

In some cases, thoughts do not become things, especially if there are misalignments in the intention. These misalignments can cancel our manifestation. For example, if you desire to be with someone who isn't available for you, then it puts a block in your manifestation because their thought is canceling yours.

Constructive interference occurs whenever waves come together so that they are in sync with each other. For two waves of equal amplitude interfering constructively, the resulting amplitude is twice as large as the amplitude of an individual wave. This is a classic example of two people in partnership thriving, whether it is in business or love.

Destructive interference occurs when waves come together in such a way that they completely cancel each other out. When two waves interfere destructively, they must have the same amplitude in opposite directions.

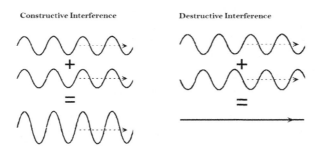

When two people align, we complement and amplify frequency.
When two people misalign, we divide and decrease frequency

Cymatics, the study of wave phenomena, demonstrates how sound and vibration influence matter at the molecular level. Water is a strong conductor of sound. Imagine how sound affects your inner workings and how it can assist in rearranging "dis-ease" into patterns of a natural state of coherence.[v]

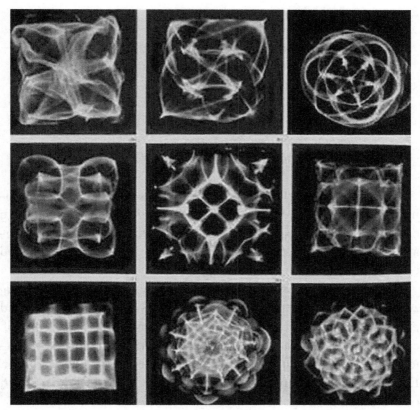

Cymatics pattern showing matter affected by sound and vibration

Dr. Emoto's study of water also proves that thoughts and feelings affect physical Reality. Written and spoken words change the expression of the water molecule. He used a very powerful microscope in a cold room and high-speed photography to photograph newly formed crystals of frozen water samples. These crystals formed in frozen water revealed changes when specific, concentrated thoughts were directed toward them. He found that the water from clear springs and the water that received loving words both showed brilliant, complex, and colorful snowflake patterns. In contrast, polluted water and water that received negative words formed incomplete, asymmetrical patterns with dull colors.[vi]

Joe Dispenza explains the difference between thought and feelings in the quantum world.

> *"If thoughts broadcast electric charges in the quantum field, and feelings broadcast magnetic charges in the quantum field, then how you feel and how you think broadcast an electromagnetic signature that influences every single atom in your life. The thought is sending the signal out, and the feeling is the magnetic charge being drawn back to you."*

Water holds information, as proven by Dr. Emoto's experiment. Our body contains 60% water. Imagine the effect we can create by talking to ourselves, whether it is positively or negatively. Therefore, we need to treat ourselves with heightened consciousness.

The documentary *Absolute Magick* suggests that *"The mind is the universal quantum crystal prison."* This means that the mind encompasses the universe within and carries the property of crystals at the sub-atomic level. The mind is linked mathematically via quantum mechanics to the wave-particle of thought. Every facet of the universe is part of the Grand Mind. In short, our mind runs the program we call the universe and life.[vii]

We can follow Lao Tzu's philosophy of creating habits from our thoughts. Let's expand here using Lao Tzu's quote,

> *"Watch your thoughts, they become words;*
> *Watch your words, they become actions;*
> *watch your actions, they become your habits;*
> *watch your habits, they become your character;*
> *watch your character, it becomes your destiny."*

Every day, our consciousness follows the principles of quantum physics. For example, if we want to make compassion a habit, the best way to do so is by making compassion a repeated effort, the same way we do when we want to physically sculpt our bodies through working out. We learn the new methodology and keep at it until it becomes a lifestyle. This is called subconscious reprogramming. This is how we reprogram our beliefs, thoughts, and DNA since we are Life Programmers.

We receive inputs from various sources, environments, media, family, and friends. There are so many inputs that weave together to develop our Reality. Our filter of discernment depends on our thoughts, beliefs, and emotions. These thoughts and emotions are rooted in triggering memories that tap into past experiences. Our output is in the form of feelings affecting our Reality, manifestation, and new experiences.

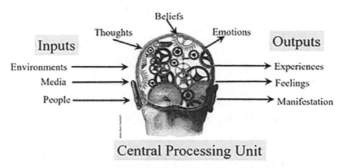

Quantum Being is processing inputs and outputs
with thoughts, beliefs, and emotions.

> *The Law of Attraction teaches us we attract
> what we are in the moment,
> not what we want from the moment.*

Our thoughts become things! If we can keep in mind the frequencies we vibrate from moment to moment, we can live a more conscious life. One thing to note is that everyone's law of attraction is individually tailored based on their circumstances, frequencies, vibrations, experiences, beliefs, etc.

Living a dream life is a manifestation and a conscious experience. We are the Weaver within making it all happen. The more aware we are of what is at play, the better off we are in making good decisions. This is how we keep weaving in the direction that best serves us towards our destiny and calling.

Thought Experiment

1. For one hour, sit and just observe your thoughts to see what type of world unfolds!
2. Document what you think via writing, drawing, or recording.
3. Notice what type of conversation you are having.
4. Make changes to the conversation if it doesn't empower you.

This experiment will ultimately affect your self-talk.

Weaver Affirmation

I am a powerful Weaver who is weaving the universe to my desired outcome for the highest potential of all the creation.

Weaver at Play

Watch your action when no one is around and genuinely feeling good.

Play music and dance without any inhibitions.

Whatever you do, is your way of weaving your beingness.

Discernment

To break free from discernment, traverse around your blocks:

Here is a simple suggestion. How about every morning you ask a question?

Start by asking:

1) How many times have you talked yourself out of a decision that might have taken you to your desired life?
2) How many times have you hesitated to speak your truth?

What decision am I not making today because I am scared to get to the life I desire?

Scan the code above with you smart phone to view
a message from Shehnaz – or follow this link:

https://youtu.be/i4mYqIm7UOM

Intelligent Architecture

The Intelligent Architect is a hidden choreographer.
-Shehnaz Soni

Thre is an innate intelligence hidden within each creation. This intelligence guides you to your next step. That is how we create our own fractal world. For example, how does a momma bird know when to kick her baby bird out of the nest? How do we know, from our gut feelings, that a person is making us feel "off"? This innate intelligence is stored in our DNA and assists us by telling us what to do next. Mystics and sages have long maintained that in this world, there is a vast interconnecting field at the roots of Reality. These roots conserve and convey information.

Who or what is the choreographer that interconnects all things visible-physical and invisible-nonphysical?

> *We are made of atoms with space in between. Since everything boils down to vibration within Zero-point field, We are less matter and more Energy.*

The reason we can't see intelligent architecture through our naked eyes is that everything appears to be dense from our perspective. The pixels on our computer screens or TV are the smallest possible indivisible form in our virtual Reality experience, and the Planck length is the smallest space between each particle in what we perceive as solid matter.

String theory proposes that at the fundamental level of our existence, we are composed of one-dimensional "strings" rather than point-like particles. These strings are vibrations in loops of string, each with its unique characteristic frequency. We see them as particles due to our illusory perception.

STRING THEORY

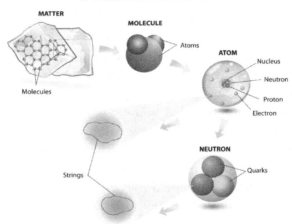

The Planck Length is the smallest between each particle. The Planck length is the smallest length at which space-time functions. In Einstein's theory, what we call space also involves time — that's why it's called space-time, because whatever it is you do to space also happens to time.

For example, Silicate mineral's crystalline structure depicts a tetrahedron triangle separated by Planck length.

It has the value = 1.62 × 10⁻³⁵m.

Silicate Minerals

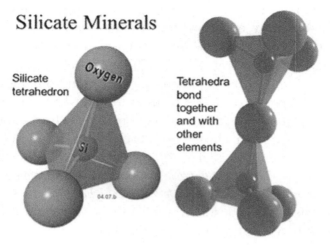

Example: Tetrahedron is formed by silicate minerals

This intelligent architecture is at the heart of understanding ourselves. By understanding this hidden architecture, you can tap into the quantum power of everything. This is why Dr. Strange and Marvel movies are so popular—we all want to create miracles. We all *can* create miracles once we understand this invisible architecture and how it forms matter. A great example of intelligent architecture at play biologically is flatworms. Flatworms are a species that regenerates on their own after being cut into two pieces. So, their design has this future action embedded into it.

An excellent example of intelligent architecture at play in life is watching a bird fly. When a bird flies in the sky, it seems like it is well-integrated with the sky, the air, and the field. Its wings and the field work together for the bird to fly to its chosen destination.

When we dance, we enjoy our breathing, our environment, and the music we are listening to. What happens to our blood when we calm down, slow our breathing, and make all our valves and capillaries work without resistance? We are in the flow with the morphogenetic field. Our cells are aligned and what we create is love throughout our body. Love is an excellent example of tapping into intelligent architecture for the benefit of all.

Scientists have been working on explaining the unified field theory and theory of everything to comprehend this invisible architecture. Unfortunately, science hasn't found the flux lines that can clearly interpret these intelligent fields.

Darwin's theory only explains our evolution from the survival of the fittest point of view. The question of what made us exist in the first place is not addressed or responded to by the theory of Darwinism. Quantum theory goes back to scientist Max Planck in the 1900s. Per Max Plank, *"All matter originates and exists only by a force which brings the particle of an atom to vibration and holds this most minute solar system of the atom together."* We must assume that there is a conscious and intelligent mind behind this force. This mind is the matrix of all matter. The invisible architecture is what exists within us and around us in the form of zero-point energy as untapped potential.

Let us explore our origin. From the *Book of Genesis*, Chapter 1: *"In the beginning, God created the Heavens and the Earth. The Earth was created without form and void. Darkness was upon the face of the deep."* This darkness highlights the timelessness of space. Darkness is the space between stars. Darkness is the substrate of all existence, where we find hidden consciousness in the form of morphogenetic fields.

What is the unified field theory that interconnects everything around us and defines whether it is matter or energy?

> *Morphogenetic fields are the closest we have come to explaining this intelligent architecture.*

Morphogenetic fields guide developing embryos into magnificent complex organisms in the form of plants, animals, and mushrooms. Rupert Sheldrake talks about this concept in detail in his book, "A New Science of Life." The Greek root word morph means to form or transform, and genesis means to come into being.

Morphogenetic fields are theorized as invisible pattern-forming agents that guide the biological process of development.[viii]

If we pull this thread consciously, we can unravel the mystery of the universe. Pythagoras shares that in the form of poetry, *"There is geometry in the humming of the strings, there is music in the spacing of the spheres."* Is this consciousness transforming itself into electromagnetic field light that further alters into the material form? This concept is prevalent in Kabbalistic teachings as well. The only visible creation we can see is in the form of an electromagnetic field.

In Kabbalah, the darkness is "Ain Soph" within the three veils on the Tree of Life.

1. The first veil, "Ain," means nothing manifested yet and is equal to zero.
2. The second veil, "Ain Soph," means in between "Nothing" and "Everything." This is where the dark matter resides, and all the possibilities exist in an unmanifest form.
3. The third veil is "Ain Soph Aur," called limitless light and is everything that is manifested from our perspective. This is equal to infinite manifestation.

Information can be divided into "in" and "formation." Ram Daas stated, "Information is just bits of data. Knowledge is putting them together. Wisdom is transcending them." We can draw information into knowledge and then into wisdom.

We can also broadcast our desires to the universe and see the universe change based on our interactions with it. For example, the word "research" is how we transform information into knowledge. We research it, that is, search it again. Through research, we gain wisdom.

Another example is Kabbalah teaching which helps me understand how light shines into my beingness and gives me a different perspective. This is knowledge. When my right ear is ringing, I know what that means based on Kabbalistic teaching. It means *"filled with understanding of its perfect law, I am guided, moment by moment, along the path of liberation."* This is wisdom.

My question to myself is, *"Where am I compromising my freedom?"* We are always paying, sometimes with money, most times with time. Energy flows where attention goes. That is why it is crucial to understand how you are choreographing your world. Ancient sacred geometric patterns symbolize how energy flows and manifests itself. Sacred geometry patterns depict matter interaction with vibrational energy. Sacred geometry patterns can be broken down into a language of mathematics that rules the entirety of our visible and invisible world.

Energetically, thoughts and images we experience in our minds stimulate neurochemical pathways in the brain. When we contemplate, this stimulation in the brain shows up in the form of sacred geometry. We open our minds to a process that takes us beyond the mundane geometry of the so-called "normal life."

> *Sacred geometry, a fabric of Reality, contains ancient secrets depicting the fundamental forms of space and time.*

Immanuel Kant, a German philosopher, connects the dots between space and time and mind and Reality; *"Space and time are the frameworks within which the mind is constrained to construct its experience of Reality."* We can leverage sacred geometry and space and time knowledge to understand God within.

Holy books like the Bible, Quran, and the Torah, have all captured the wisdom of ancient knowledge. Sixteen hundred years ago, St. Augustine said, *"The universe was brought into being in a less than fully formed state which was gifted to transform itself from unformed matter into a truly marvelous array of structure and life forms."* We finally understand this concept spoken about 1600 years ago. In this way, life is mathematically formed in perfect continuity with its surroundings via complex design.

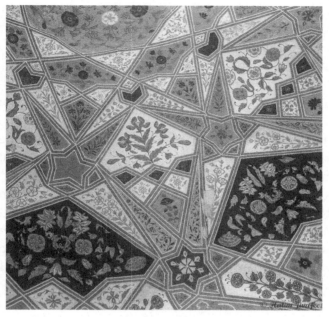

Sacred geometry depicted in an Islamic Mosque; a photo taken by my dad.

The energy that manifests itself obeys specific universal laws. The famous *Heisenberg Uncertainty Principle* states that you can't simultaneously discern both the momentum and position of a particle since the matter is always in formation within the physical world. For example, a crystal is formed via a wave-like spiraling motion. Everything we are exposed to has an energetic signature and frequency that impacts our energetic balance. This means all humans have the same properties as crystals; the ability to amplify, absorb, store, and transmit a range of vibrational energies.[ix]

Crystal

How can the science of crystals unravel the correct understanding of matters misinterpreted as Magick? The documentary *Absolute Magick* explains the answer. In *Absolute Magick*, the universe is described as being created in the form of a matrix, crystal-like structure via a series of strings and lattices. Over time, trillions of these cells are linked together in a spiraling motion. They are stacked layer upon layer until the crystal is formed. For example, mandalas are visual depictions of crystals building one layer upon another.

Quartz crystal begins its life deep within the Earth from hot vapor. Hot vapor is a supersaturated solution of silicon dioxide. As the solution cools down, a cell unit of quartz forms in the same way that an oyster forms its pearl. The forming atoms bond where there is the most energy. This matrix of creation are forms built one on top of the other. This primary cell unit attracts other silicon dioxide molecules in order for the multiplication to continue.

This formation takes the shape of a tetrahedron molecule composed of four atoms of oxygen, with one silicon atom suspended within. Quantum Gravity Research has been working on a unified field theory called emergence theory. Emergence theory is also known as E8 theory or "An Exceptionally Simple Theory of Everything." E8 theory proves, via the quasicrystal concept, that everything comes into existence via the basic shape of a tetrahedron. A quasicrystal is a structure that is ordered but not periodic. Quasicrystals can project higher dimension information to explain how matter is formed through the sacred geometry of the tetrahedron. Quasicrystals have been used in surgical instruments, LED lights, and non-stick frying pans. They have poor heat conductivity, which makes them good insulators.[x,xi]

A tetrahedron (equilateral triangles like a pyramid) is the basic geometric shape that creates our Reality based on the Pythagoras Theorem. A tetrahedron is the most efficient geometrical shape to hold fractal energy. The state of each tetrahedron, the lowest geometric form, combines to affect our bifurcation. Our decision stems from our perception, and our perception is affected by the Reality we are experiencing moment to moment.

When I was in a relationship that was not aligning with my true calling, I would have continued going downhill without a course correction. That is why we should ask the critical question during challenging times, *"does this path align with my destiny?"*

We are influencing our destiny based on every action we take, moment by moment. The structure we build with a cascading tetrahedron in the material form is how we affect our manifestation and destiny. Thoughts become things, and things become us. We are building intelligent architecture through our built-in quantum processing.

Memory

The word Memory can be broken down into:

Mem + Ore=Water (in Hebrew) + Valuable matter (Crystal)

Crystals hold the blueprint of the living consciousness records contained in the evolutionary histories of the Earth and beyond. Crystals record the experiences of all life that have been imprinted through the complex patterns of frequencies and mathematical coding.

We are built with water and crystals. This is why we have a memory. We have memory to help us not repeat negative patterns and keep the ones that serve. Consciousness runs on probable yet unpredictable and indeterminate systems, proven by quantum physics. Our access to memory at will is why we experience everything in a linear fashion. If we erase our memory, how do we learn from our mistakes?

There are two types of memory:

<u>Intrinsic Memory:</u>

One type of Intrinsic memory is hardwired into us via our DNA.

Our DNA stores data just like crystal. A bioengineer and geneticist at Harvard's Wyss Institute successfully stored 5.5 petabits of data — around 700 terabytes — in a single gram of DNA! Instead of binary data being encoded as magnetic regions on a hard drive platter, strands of DNA that store 96 bits are synthesized, with each of the bases (TGAC) representing a binary value (T and G = 1, A and C = 0).

To read the data stored in DNA, you need to sequence it — just as if you were sequencing the human genome — and convert each of the TGAC bases back into binary. This means that all of your memories are stored within you and accessible by your brain and body. Decoding and encoding are only needed for the human brain to comprehend these messages beyond binary numbers.

DNA as a storage medium is unique since it means we don't need a special environment to keep data intact for thousands of years. Of course, individual humans don't live for thousands of years. So, what does all of this mean for you? This means that *all* of your memories are stored within you and accessible by your brain and body at will.[xii]

Our DNA also stores information about how often we have used our muscles for specific movements, connecting our DNA to the ultimate entropy and aging of humans. In the aerospace engineering world, we call this the "service life" information contained within each flight article.

For example, I prayed five times a day as a good Muslim girl growing up. Over the last 22 years, I have not prayed five times daily; however, I can still recall all the Arabic prayers. This information is considered internal memory stored within my DNA.

What is this innate intelligence that repairs and regenerates DNA? Innate intelligence can enable you to meet your heart's desire if you allow yourself that kind of love. In the movie "Finding Nemo," the fish discover that working together by swimming downward as a group is the only way to break away from the fish net cast by humans. This act of love depicted by all the fish is a type of innate intelligence. This form of love for others helps us break free from systematic enslavement.

Teamwork is the key to making your dream work.

One of my visionary friends once told me, *"No matter how incredible one person is by himself or herself, when we combine the incredibleness of the group, it will always exceed the incredibleness of one person."*

Our cells, just like the fish, can be self-aligned for a purpose. This understanding is key to how we can reprogram our DNA. A DNA upgrade will not make us look drastically different. We go through minuscule changes so minute that we can only feel the changes we make every nanosecond. Relativity is how we feel the change or motion that is at play at all times since we are moving molecules with a space in between. We do not necessarily see the changes unless we can perform time-lapse photography. This is a technique in photography in which the frequency at which film frames are captured is much lower than the frequency used to view the sequence.

> *The other Intrinsic memory is the one we access via our consciousness by tapping into Akashic fields.*

For example, when we visit a place that looks familiar, this familiarity may be due to our stored memory through experiences we had during living many lives. When we ask a question, we have the answer. We are only uncovering the information by asking the right question. For example, you decide to become a pilot, and when you take your first lesson, you feel that you have done this before. People who believe in reincarnation can easily relate to this. Even if you don't believe in reincarnation, you can experiment by doing something you love. The reason you are gravitating to it in the first place is because of your familiarity.

External Memory:

Crystal is an excellent example of an external memory storage device. Crystals are configured just like any other matter in the universe, with a lot more space in between than meets the eyes.

All things vibrate, including crystals. Stimulating a crystal makes it vibrate or synchronize, and crystals "sing" to the harmony of the vibration. This means vibratory information or energy in different frequencies can be stored inside an empty space, just like memory. Therefore, a vast amount of data can be stored and harnessed in the dark matter of a crystal.

> *Dark matter is powerful but invisible to the naked eye, and all crystals contain dark matter.*

Dark matter is called "dark" because it does not appear to interact with the electromagnetic field, which means it does not absorb, reflect, or emit electromagnetic radiation (like light) and is, therefore, difficult to detect.

> *Dark matter brings light into our consciousness.*

While we are asleep, the dark matter of our unconscious mind mirrors this process via a dream. It highlights issues hidden within our subconscious mind. Can we stimulate the dark matter of the universe to unveil its deep dark secret? If we can, are we performing Magick? We can do that merely by thinking and tapping into the unconscious world since thoughts become things.

Similarly, a hologram is another excellent example of an external memory storage device. In a hologram, billions of bits of information in binary form can be stored in a tiny space. In the movie "Superman," Superman receives a message from his deceased parents informing him about his origin via crystal holographs. These holographs have a quantum memory.

Just like Superman's parents used their extraordinary power to communicate outside the space-time continuum, we also have a similar extraordinary power to communicate in our bones and DNA because they are piezoelectric. Piezoelectricity, a reversible process, converts mechanical energy into electrical energy. For example, clapping can turn lights on using piezoelectricity. Piezoelectric properties are the reason quartz crystal has electric charges and makes it useful for communication.

A crystal's capacity to store information, combined with piezoelectricity, is why we use them in the building of mobile phones, radios, television, quartz watches, microphones, guitar amplifiers, and rockets that take us beyond the Earth's atmosphere. Crystals, being quantum amplifiers, are used in temples to magnify sound.

A Quantum Being is as powerful as any rocket I have designed.

Human Versus Rocket

- Both humans and rockets are dependent on structures/ skeletons to provide shape, strength, efficiency, and maneuverability.
- Both are vehicles with an outer skin that protects and contains all the major functions intact, providing a thermal protection system.
- Both are affected by the mass it carries since it affects their functionality.
- Human brain = rocket avionics subsystem.
- Quartz crystal is widely used within electronics as high-performance resonators in filters and oscillators. Humans have crystals inside their brains and organs.
- Human will = rocket power.
- Both have electrical systems built in to carry messages through the brain or avionics subsystem.
- Both have built-in redundancy, like a human has two kidneys etc.
- Both are affected by external radiation

- Both are designed to run in an electromagnet environment
- Both have tubes/cables to carry fluid throughout the body.
- Both have sensors/cell receptors.
- The human engine runs on water, and rockets run on liquid hydrogen and liquid oxygen; both are constituents of water.
- Plumbing is delicate in both cases; refer to our heart.

You may have heard stories of the crystal skull that helps anyone who wants information by tapping into the memory it holds due to the ancient nature of its origin.

I experienced crystal skull readings in 2013 when facing a major fork in the road in my life. I felt very powerful during my interaction with the crystal skull. I had a telepathic communication that flowed between me and the crystal skull without any resistance. I asked a question, and I got a response without delay or hesitation. It was a wonderful Magickal experience.

Crystal skulls embody Metatron's cube, an emergence from the Flower of Life pattern that contains every geometric shape that exists in the universe. When non-physical matter, in the form of thought, emotions, and aura, interacts with physical matter, an emerging pattern is created based on the vibrational energy in the Flower of Life pattern.

Flower of Life

The Flower of Life (FOL) is called sacred architecture because it underlies everything woven into the fabric of all creation. Archaeologists have found the "Flower of Life" symbol all over the world, including in Ireland, Turkey, Israel, Japan, Egypt, China, Germany, India, and England. The oldest known depictions of the Flower of Life were found in the Temple of Osiris in Egypt.

I visited Abydos, Egypt, in October 2019 and got an opportunity to experience the sacred symbols of the Flower of Life in person. Below is the picture of two Flower of Life symbols taken during my visit. The symbol is faint but clear and precise. The FOL symbol is burned into, not carved or etched, at the atomic structure of the rock via an extraordinary technology not comprehensible to us even in the 20ᵗʰ century.

The Flower of Life design is replicated in the rock in Abydos, Egypt (the picture was taken by my camera)

The Flower of Life symbol dates back to at least 6000 years ago. Recent research has concluded that the first symbol could not have been made earlier than 535 Before Christ (BC).

Dr. Nasim Haramein, who has spent more than 30 years researching and discovering connections in quantum mechanics, asks, *"How did humans in 535 BC know about the Flower of Life geometry of the overlapping spherical Planck scale oscillating wave-forms that make up the proton and therefore all atoms, and therefore all matter in the universe?"*

The term Planck scale refers to quantities of space, time, energy, and other units similar in magnitude to corresponding Planck units. In other words, how did ancient humans know the high-level math needed to burn the flower of life symbol into their art and architecture? The answer is they didn't need to "know" it in the usual sense. The knowledge was within their DNA, and they were tapping into this knowledge store consciously or unconsciously.[xiii]

Would you be shocked if I told you that solid matter doesn't exist? It's true! We only see rigidity in matter because of the togetherness of atoms.

We think of the world as made up of particles held together by forces, but quantum theory tells us that matter is just a mess of fields that are Planck length apart and properly described by invoking the mathematics of quantum physics. Realization of this constant state of fluctuation in matter means there is a continual opportunity for change.

Since you are reading this book hoping to effect change in your life, this fact should give you hope! Nasim Haramein says it well, *"You can think of space like this fluid of quantum fluctuation."* Atomic structure is composed of oscillating energy grids surrounded by other oscillating grids orbiting at very high speeds. These grids are affected by constant motion and interactions.

Dr. Stuart Hammeroff, an American anesthesiologist who has been studying consciousness for 30 years, elaborates on how Planck-scale geometry is at the heart of our Reality.

> *"I imagine the Planck scale as a complex geometric pattern that is fractal in nature, capable of repeating itself at higher scales and sizes. Embedded in that geometric quantum pattern are the presumably irreducible components of Reality, the basic building blocks of existence. Physics says that fundamental properties of matter such as spin, mass, and charge are irreducible components of the universe that are somehow embedded in this Planck scale geometry."*

This knowledge makes it clear how matter is formed and unformed and how illusory the world can be when you truly understand it from a quantum physics perspective.[xiv]

To better understand consciousness and our relationship to it, let us take a journey into how the FOL pattern emerged.

Imagine consciousness floating in a void represented by a "dot."

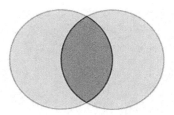

A circled dot was used by the Pythagoreans to represent the first metaphysical being, the Monad. Monad refers to the supreme being, divinity, or the totality of all things. Monad is an indivisible, ultimately simple entity, such as an atom, a person, or a spirit. We can call Monad a sentient being, one with the faculty of sensation and the power to perceive, reason, and think.[xv]

This spirit (intelligent and conscious energy) has an innate circle of influence and awareness. This causes a need for interaction, and the spirit needs something to move relative to itself. You are probably familiar with Isaac Newton's third law that states for every action (force) in nature, there is an equal and opposite reaction. In other words, if object A exerts a force on object B, then object B also exerts an equal and opposite force on object A. This is how we interact with our consciousness; thus, another circle gets created. Two circles are self-aware and identical. Conscious interaction is the key to creation.

The creation of a second circle symbolized the start of the duality of God and Goddess. Duality is all around us; Yin/Yang, dark/light, love/hate, etc. This duality exists in us as we depict masculine and feminine aspects within ourselves. We have right hemisphere-feminine qualities and left hemisphere-masculine qualities.

We are in constant motion. We have to breathe to stay alive. All life exists in a waveform, and we feel the waveform in the form of energy. We breathe into the patternistic waveform containing a sinusoidal curve (periodically going positive and negative). The everyday sun rises and sets. We have happy feelings and sad feelings. Everything visible to our eye can be explained by waveform. Feel your breath in and then out. We are making a waveform with our breathing.

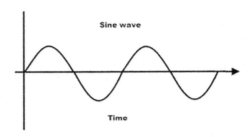

In the Egyptian temple, this squiggle-lined symbol is very common. It depicts serpent energy in the form of a wave that indicates electrical energy, also known as kundalini energy. Kundalini energy is intertwined in our spine, signifying the duality within us.

An artistic interpretation of duality with intertwining serpents. A depiction of the kundalini energy within us that travels from the base chakra of our spine to the crown chakra at the top of our head.

Duality is embedded in everything. Control and letting go are intertwined as well. The best strategy is to let it go. In letting go, we get more control of the situation.

> *Momentum only occurs when you let it go.*

When I was deciding to choose a career path versus being a homemaker, I had to avail both sides of my brain to make the decision. I have always wanted to prove my independence to the patriarchal culture; that as a *woman*, I can still be successful in a man's world. Hence, I picked a profession that is very male-dominated and still succeeded. I wanted to experience both roles as a mother and a scientist. I chose to keep my corporate job because financial freedom was a high priority for me. In the process, I became a role model for my kids by showing them a mother who enjoys work and spending quality time with them when not working.

The image formed by two intersecting circles is called Vesica Pisces, a model that symbolizes the womb of creation. This symbol is represented in our eyes and our female genitalia. Vesica Pisces depicts the union and fusion of two and was availed in the design of the Great Pyramid of Giza. Tantric sex is an excellent example of a powerful union that can enhance the experience of two humans coming together by affecting each other with intense energies.

As above so below. The Flower of Life pattern is formed at the seed level to create a quantum being, similar to how everything around us comes into existence. These patterns are created automatically because of our built-in intelligence.

Our consciousness in action continues to result in spirit interactions – actions we take because we are sentient beings and can't stand still. Therefore, we keep making overlapping circles, resulting in seven intersecting circles. These interactions are performed at various levels of our existence.

Seven is a sacred number that depicts deep introspective, intuitive secrets to the outer world of phenomena, but to the inner worlds, of secrecy, intrigue, and hidden mysteries. This seven-circle is called the "See/Egg of Life" symbol. In human pregnancy, a developing fetus is considered an embryo until the ninth week. The shape of the Egg of Life is said to be the same of a multicellular embryo in its first hours of creation.

These patterns are called the blueprint of God, like God's unique thumbprint we see in our fingerprints. Through ratcheting (putting into motion) and spinning the Seed/Egg of Life, we get Tube Torus. Tube Torus is referred to as toroidal flow. This ratcheting process is a natural phenomenon at work at all times. We are only a conduit to it.

As we continue the interactions beyond seven circles, we can create the Flower of Life. It is composed of 19 circles. The Fruit of Life is another circular pattern we can create. Thirteen circles lifted away from the Flower of Life pattern make the Fruit of Life. Thirteen circles represent the 13 knowledge systems. This is the source of all that exists. Each one explains another aspect of Reality. The 13 knowledge systems are also the key to unity and transition between worlds and dimensions. For those who are musically inclined and play the chromatic scale of the 12 notes, are you aware that the 13th note is actually repeating the first note, only on a higher frequency? When you attain a higher octave, you enter a higher dimension!

This 13-circle symbol provides the geometric basis for delineating Metatron's cube, which brings forth the platonic solids. Can you see the dazzling creations formed simply by a single spiritual interaction?

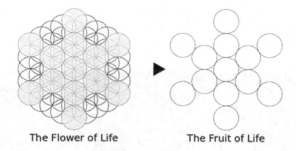

The Flower of Life   The Fruit of Life

Here we have a perfect example of the intersection of science and spirituality. Metatron was an Archangel mentioned in all books of religion, according to Egyptian Thoth Hermes. Astonishingly, Metatron's cube contains *all* five key sacred patterns or shapes that make up *all* matter in this universe. Known as the Platonic solids, these shapes are:

1.   Star tetrahedron
2.   Hexahedron/cube
3.   Octahedron
4.   Dodecahedron
5.   Icosahedron

Four of these Platonic solids are the archetypal patterns behind the four elements in *all* of Creation; earth, fire, air, and water. The fifth pattern is considered the universal substance of creation, and in some Mystery Schools, was considered the fifth element of aether or ether. The fifth solid is the dodecahedron. Tesla's experiment reveals the existence of aether or ether. *"The aether is an ever-present field that connects all things. The nonphysical force behind all physical phenomenon."*

Crystals are sacred geometric forms based on Platonic solids. Can you see how the most basic elements of our natural and scientific world are perfectly aligned and integrated with the spiritual world?

In the 1980s, Professor Robert Moon at the University of Chicago suggested that the entire periodic table of elements is based on the Platonic solids.

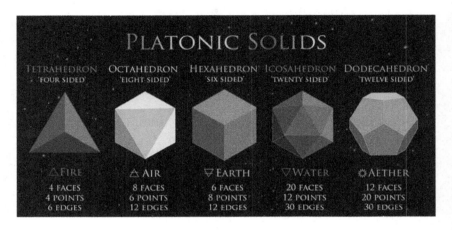

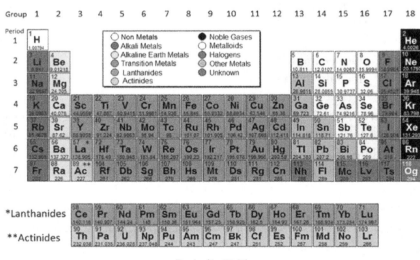

Periodic Table

The periodic table is taught in school to understand basic concepts such as water being comprised of two atoms of hydrogen and one atom of oxygen. We already know that periodic table elements exist in our human body. For example, roughly 96% of the mass of the human body is made up of *just* four elements: oxygen, carbon, hydrogen, and nitrogen, with much of that in the form of water. The remaining 4% is a sparse sampling of the periodic table of elements. These nutrients perform various functions, including building bones and cell structures, regulating the body's pH, carrying electrical charges, and driving chemical reactions. This is why the Ayurveda principle works when applied to heal the body. Ayurveda accounts for all five elements (air, fire, earth, water, and aether) within our body and is a practice that is informed by material Reality.[xvi]

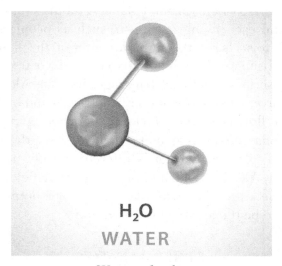

Water molecules

Tube Torus

Each atom and everything on the planet are surrounded by its own energy field known as the torus. This self-sustaining, balanced, and dynamic energy flow process is the base for everything powerful on the planet, consisting of a single axis and two vortices. Energy passes through one vortex, along the center of the axis, out the other vortex, wraps back around the circumference, and renews by passing through the original vortex.

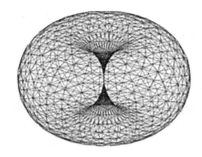

This shape can be clearly seen in some of nature's most powerful creations: the tornado, the whirlpool, the black hole, magnetic fields, energy fields around planets and the sun, etc. It is also found around each living organism, such as people and plants. The Earth's torus is run through the center of the planet and creates our atmosphere. Torus contains a code of vortex energy that uniquely describes light and language, like the Akashic record (aka the "universal supercomputer" and the "Mind of God").

Toroidal flow is a cloud of charge depicted by plasma. Most scientists today agree that more than 99% of the universe is composed of plasma. Plasma is interchangeably used as zero-point energy, Akashic field, and morphogenetic field. All plasma domains have a toroidal form, like a torus or a donut. Plasma is considered to be the fourth state of matter.

STATES OF MATTER

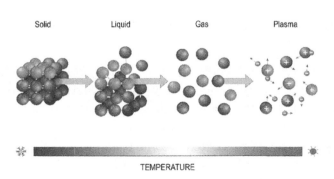

Plasma atoms are divided into free-floating negative electrons and positive ions (an atom that has lost its electrons). Plasma is sometimes called ionized gas.

> *The reason why plasma fields choose to manifest themselves in this profound toroidal form is that they had to find a self-sustaining, self-organizing recursive geometry to optimize their survival energy.*

This is yet another example of current science revealing spiritual truths that have been passed down for eons. Recent scientific discoveries have proven that the torus field is very real. The torus field is also known as the zero-point Akashic field or the "A field" and is the source of all things that arise in time and space. It is also the constant and enduring memory of the universe. The zero-point Akashic field holds a record of everything that has happened in life, on Earth, and in the cosmos and relates it to all that is yet to happen.

Our heart is our most important asset and a source of the tremendous amount of energy we have to offer to the world. This is why, when our heart stops, we die. The Heart Math Institute, developers of a science-based, heart-focused breathing meditation, has proven that the heart's electromagnetic frequency arcs out from the heart and back in the form of a torus field. The axis of this heart torus extends from the pelvic floor to the top of the skull.

The whole field is holographic, meaning that information about it can be read from each and every point in the torus. The heart emits an electromagnetic field that extends outwards in every direction from the body. That is why we feel the presence of others around us when they are in close proximity. So, yes, it is scientifically possible to fill your heart with love and radiate this love to the world around you!

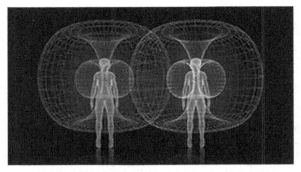

Our invisible electromagnetic fields radiate outward from
our hearts to others and vice-versa via Tube Torus

Heal your Heart --> Create a Better Home life -->
Create a Better World

Home is referred to as the liberation from the slavery
we have placed ourselves in, a "Golden Cage."

The morphogenetic field sends energy and information to the brain, every cell in the body, and into the Earth's global electromagnetic field.

Therefore, we are always affecting ourselves and everything around us. These influences come in the form of waves, gravity, energy, and light affecting the entire universe. When sound is in motion, it creates a toroidal field/magnetic field, which creates electromagnetic force. Magnetism, a physical phenomenon produced by the motion of electric charge, results in attractive and repulsive forces between objects. This phenomenon is at the heart of all interconnections, hence the word magnet.

Gravity, electromagnetism, light, and time
are interlinked and intertwined.

The sea itself moves with the gravitational push and pull of the moon, and it is part of a greater whole being pulled by the wave-like force of gravity.

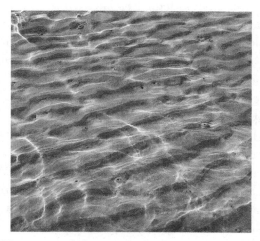

The waves of the sea moving in response to the gravitational forces of the universe

There is a story of a sailor and professor riding together in a boat. The professor asked the sailor, *"Do you know about the galaxy and solar system and the universe?"*

The sailor responded, *"No, I have no clue about it."*

The professor replied, *"You have wasted 25% of your life by not knowing the fundamentals of our existence."*

They rode a little further, and the professor asked the sailor again, *"Have you traveled the world and seen the seven wonders of the world?"*

The sailor responded, *"No, I haven't traveled anywhere."*

The professor responded, *"You have wasted 50% of your life by not visiting the most amazing places."*

They rode a little further, and the professor asked the sailor again, *"Do you know biology, ecology, zoology, geography, and physiology?"*

The sailor responded, *"No, I have no clue about it."*

The professor replied, *"You have wasted 75% of your life by not understanding the basics of our life."*

After a while, the sailor asked the professor, *"Do you know how to swim?"* The professor responded, *"No."*

The sailor stated, *"Professor, you are about to waste 100% of your life since this boat has a hole, and we are about to sink."*

So, all the knowledge and wisdom in the world won't help you if you don't know how to apply it practically in the real world.

If you feel overwhelmed by the vastness of the science that underpins all spiritual principles, keep in mind that it will make more sense as you begin to put those principles into practice.

Remember the Flower of Life? The Flower of Life is a knowledge system that should be taught in schools. The Flower of Life is a timeless geometric form that makes up all that exists! It is the fundamental geometry from which Reality emerges. It is, in fact, a diagram of the unified field theory from an ancient knowledge system. It is also a geometric map to seeing God in everything. The more you look into it, the more incredible this concept becomes.

The Fruit of Life is said to be the *blueprint* of the universe, containing the basis for the design of every atom, molecular structure, life form, and everything in existence.

This understanding of how everything in life is choreographed beautifully and with extraordinary attention to detail—a level of detail that is incomprehensible at times—is how you upgrade your DNA.

What is this innate intelligence that repairs and regenerates DNA?

> ### *DNA is our key to opening the door to being a quantum human.*

DNA is an intelligent molecule that encodes the complete set of genetic instructions (the genome) required to gather, maintain, and reproduce every living being. In the book, The Spark in the Machine, Dr. Daniel Keown highlights the fact that *"the human body is a perfect example of a system where its characteristics are more than its parts- has science ever isolated the cells responsible for a smile? We know it won't because a smile is a product of wholeness-there are no smile cells."* So there are organizing centers like Morphogenetic fields that instruct specific cells in DNA to mindfully generate and connect protein sequences to become the unique structure in the form, which we then see as an ultimate existence of quantum beings. The genetic code is sometimes called the universal code because it is used by nearly all living organisms on Earth.

The genetic code is the instructions cells use to translate information from genetic material (DNA or mRNA) into amino acids. There are 64 codons in the mRNA code, each codon consisting of three nucleotides. The three-letter nature of codons means that the four nucleotides found in mRNA — A, U, G, and C — can produce a total of 64 (4 *4*4) different combinations. Of these 64 codons, 61 represent amino acids, and the remaining three represent stop signals, which trigger the end of protein synthesis.

Amino acids are strung together and modified to build proteins. These proteins carry a wide range of roles in the body. Once a protein is complete, it has a job to perform. Some proteins are enzymes that catalyze biochemical reactions. Other proteins play roles in DNA replication and transcription. Yet other proteins provide structural support for the cell, create channels through the cell membrane, or carry out one of many other crucial cellular support functions. Keeping our DNA in check is key to showing up the best we can in this world.

This is why epigenetics work. Epigenetics is the study of how your behaviors and environment cause changes that affect the way your genes work. Unlike genetic changes, epigenetic changes are reversible. They do not change your DNA sequence but can change how your body reads a DNA sequence.

An affirmation can be a powerful way to program our subconscious and upgrade our DNA. This is how we can conquer hereditary diseases.

By virtue of surviving, we end up evolving. When we get a severe disease that knocks us off our path, we upgrade our DNA at the soul level and come back stronger than before. When you understand there is a self-sustaining principle at play at all times in the form of torus energy creating a Flower of Life pattern, you will feel more empowered when facing difficult life and health challenges.

Self-Sustainment is at the heart of the all-natural phenomenon. Human is emitting Carbon Di Oxide. Tree is absorbing Carbon Di Oxide. Human is absorbing Oxygen. Tree is emitting Oxygen.

Here I am, by my house in Huntsville, AL, experiencing all the goodness of the outdoor energy emitted from the wind, air, water, and trees

The sacred geometry of the Flower of Life expresses our connection to spirit and the outside world. When we understand this architecture of our beingness, we create harmony within ourselves.

I have been implementing the Flower of Life for 12 years now. My life in this time has drastically changed. I was an unhappy wife with four boys 12 years ago. Now I am sharing my wisdom with the world and living a happier life with my four boys exhibiting more freedom and knowledge than before.

Here is a summary of what we have learned in this chapter:

➢ Everything in formation can be expressed by elements in the periodic table.

➢ Everything in the periodic table can be explained by the Flower of Life pattern.

➢ Everything in the Flower of Life pattern can be explained by the consciousness that creates our Reality.

➢ Ancient wisdom recognized that these small patterns in the Flower and Fruit of Life represented the building blocks that were the blueprint for *everything* in the universe.

➢ A seed, after all, contains all the material needed to become a mighty tree, regardless of the size of the tree.

➢ A crystal matrix gets created around a seed point, just like the Flower of Life patterns.

➢ Our DNA holds the key to our intelligent architecture.

Do you see now how the Flower of Life contains all knowledge systems to transform light (knowledge) into matter (quantum being)? When you comprehend the Flower of Life, you upgrade your DNA and affect your transformation.

Using this knowledge, we can be confident when we interact that we are creating a dynamic that permeates all aspects of our lives. If we can pay attention to our dynamics with others and act according to our emotions and feelings, we can help bring more harmony to the world as a whole.

Now that you are aware of how much knowledge is embedded in your quantum human self, you can choose to follow what you *know* rather than what you *think*. You are responsible for your experiences and your feelings, and you can take a more proactive role in creating the experiences and feelings you want just by tuning in to your relationship dynamics.

We affect our ongoing manifestation by tapping into the beautiful tapestry of this intelligent architecture, following a sacred geometry of things to come. When we engulf ourselves in the activity of creating art, we are upgrading our DNA by moving our eyes and hands in the art of creation. This is why Leonardo da Vinci drew and studied this beautiful pattern and its mathematical properties. As quantum beings, we are the living embodiment of the sacred geometry of the Flower of Life.

DNA Stimulation Exercise

We can stimulate our DNA by indulging in activities that can decrypt the data from the stored memory of the Akashic record and bring forth your stored awareness so you can exercise wisdom:

1. Pick an image of any type that grabs your attention, for example, Tarot cards.
2. Ask a question from your heart.
3. See what message you are picking up intuitively based on your sacred architecture of life at that particular moment.
4. Self-reflect and ponder to see if it all makes sense.

Integration Exercise

Integrating all aspects of each moment is the key to living in the present and availing your light in present circumstances. This will lead to greater future experiences and manifestations.

1. What disappointments are making you fearful about the future? List them one by one.

2. Imagine you are going to the deepest part of a forest where there is a wooden chest lying on the ground.
3. Put all your disappointments listed in step 1 inside the wooden chest.
4. Bury the wooden chest in the ground
5. Breathe and be aware that you are in a state of quantum being.
6. Let it all go!

What you resists persists, so let us not resist.
Instead, integrate what you feel with what you know.

Scan the code above with you smart phone to view a message from Shehnaz – or follow this link:

https://youtu.be/TY6VZ45G8xA

Flight Three

Soul Activation

Chapter 9

Step into Your Light

When you step into the light, you get all the attention you command, and Magick unfolds.

-Shehnaz Soni

s Einstein's theory of relativity explains, if you were to travel at the speed of light, then strange things would happen to space and time. You would experience being in all places and times at once. You would, in other words, be eternal. Let us look at this from the perspective of light. When the world was created and the first light came into being, the entirety of space and time was created and held in a single moment. This means that light is the reason we see everything, hence the phrase, *"Let us shed some light on it."*

Light is information, and so is the dark. This is the key to a conscious being. Light is trapped in the form of matter. Dark matter is impossible to detect; however, this is where the experience hides until it shows itself in the form of light. As Carl Jung said, *"As far as we can discern, the sole purpose of human existence is to kindle a light in the darkness of mere being."*

Therefore, light is the key to understanding how the physical world reveals itself. The Book of Genesis says," *The Spirit of God moved upon the face of the waters. And God said, 'Let there be light,' and then, there was light.*" Light is a critical ingredient in our life that brings everything into existence. Light particles travel to our eyes along light waves via the electromagnetic force. The electromagnetic force is carried by electromagnetic fields composed of electric fields and magnetic fields, and it is responsible for electromagnetic radiation such as light. There is an interaction occurring between electricity and magnetism. This is how our universe depicts a form and shows up as a solid, dense Reality.

Therefore, light affects our Reality. If you have an imagination, you see things, and that is because the light is emanating through your imagination to affect your Reality. For example, when I visited a museum in Arkansas in 2009 called "The Museum of Discovery," my husband and I decided to test our energies by being in the room called "Mind/Body/Spirit." There was a metallic ball placed in the center of the table, and the goal was to see which party could attract the ball and keep it on their side for the entire time. I won the game, to my husband's surprise. He later asked me what my secret was. In my imagination, I had gone into my meditation altar, a very serene and calming place in my mind. I had put myself in a state of peace through my imagination. This is how I created a state of coherence and aligned all my cells to focus on being serene. Magick unfolded in the form of meeting my intentions of keeping the metallic ball close to me. There are so many ways we can apply this learning for the result we want to achieve in our life.

How can we be so naive that we think that *"what we see is all there is"*? Bruce Lipton says it simply, *"What quantum physics teaches us is that everything we thought was physical is not physical."* Why? Because we believed truth was only seen through physical existence and disregarded all other feelings we couldn't see or prove. We all have heard the phrase, "Love is blind." Love is an electrifying feeling that you experience and want to continue to experience. This feeling is invisible to us and others, yet we all feel it. If you are blind, you don't see anything, but you can feel it. Matter is dense, and so you sense it.

A 2020 article written in *Futurism*, explains how invisible aliens can live on Earth. Aliens could be living in a microscopic "shadow biosphere." These aliens could have silicon-based biochemistry, as opposed to carbon-based. "This means we can't study or even notice them because they are outside our frequency band."[xvii]

A depiction of aliens roaming in a shadow biosphere on Earth

You might be surprised to know that most of the universe is filled with matter that emits no light, no infrared heat, no radio waves, and no radiation. The lights we see are a tiny fraction of the electromagnetic spectrum. Our eyes only see a limited range of colors since these ranges make up a fraction of the total sound and light frequency range.

➢ Our eyes can only see between the 430-770 Terahertz range.
➢ Our ears can only detect sound between 20-20,000 HZ.

ELECTROMAGNETIC SPECTRUM

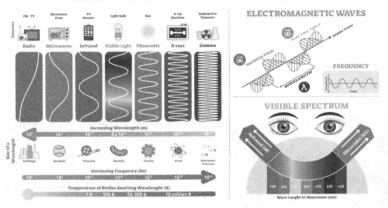

Wide range of the electromagnetic spectrum

Comparatively, dogs, cats, rats, and rabbits have very poor color vision, while bees and butterflies can see colors we can't see. Evolution led bees to adopt ultraviolet vision because flowers leave scattered ultraviolet patterns. The ultraviolet vision allows the insects to easily identify targets and pollinate. Even though humans can't see colors beyond our visible spectrum, we can build machines that can. This is what spectrometers are for.

We experience negative feelings when surrounded by unnatural electromagnetic fields that emanate from radios, TVs, microwaves, 5G towers, or X-rays. We experience positive feelings when surrounded by natural electromagnetic Earth energies in the form of Schumann resonance of 7.83 Hz frequencies. Schumann's resonance, sometimes called "Earth's heartbeat," induces a brain state that helps us relax, heal, and perceive and experience Earth energies. Schumann resonance frequencies are very important for our health. That is why we have to create a balance between our exposure to positive and negative feelings.

We Emit Light

Past research has shown that the human body emits mostly infrared and electromagnetic radiation with a frequency lower than visible light. *Live Science* published an article on July 22nd, 2009, proving our human body consists of light. Scientists in Japan employed immensely sensitive cameras capable of detecting single photons. Light energy is released in the form of a photon. Photons are emitted when electrons move from one energy state to another. The name photon derives from the Greek word for light, and its symbol is the gamma-ray.

Five healthy male volunteers in their 20s were placed bare-chested in front of the cameras. They were in complete darkness in light-tight rooms for 20 minutes every three hours from 10 a.m. to 10 p.m. for three days. From this experiment, scientists revealed that the human body glows, emitting visible light in extremely small quantities at levels that rise and fall with the day.[xviii]

The researchers found this body glow rose and fell throughout the day, suggesting that light emission is linked to our body clocks and follows circadian rhythms, most likely due to how our metabolic rhythms fluctuate throughout the day. Researcher Hitoshi Okamura, a circadian biologist in Japan, suggests that cameras that can spot weak emissions could help spot medical conditions. The body's hormonal reaction to light wavelengths regulates our circadian rhythm, affecting our cognition, blood pressure, immune system, metabolism, and sleep and wake cycles.

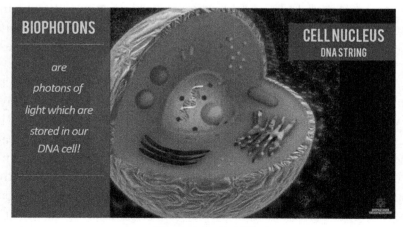

Biophotons in cell

Dr. Olivia Bader-Lee, psychologist and energy healer, emphasizes the natural healing process in her practice. She says, *"Humans can absorb biophotons and heal through other humans, animals, and any part of nature."* That's why our physical bodies become a sponge when soaked in a natural, serene environment. Being soaked in nature and Earth's electromagnetic fields (EMF) is the best way to enhance our health since our body absorbs biophoton light from the Sun through the skin and eyes. German Physicist Fritz-Albert proved the existence of biophotons in all living organisms. Biophotons are produced through a biological system by the DNA molecules in our cells.[xix]

Trees and nature emit biophotons that are nurturing to our soul and mind. That is why we feel rejuvenated when we take a walk outside. We get our nourishment through biophotons from nature. Our cells have the photovoltaic property of converting sunlight into electricity. This is how we provide more power to our human craft. Biophotons become the fuel our body needs for nourishment.

There is a scientific paper titled *Emission of Mitochondrial Biophotons and their Effect on Electrical'* explaining the interaction of biophotons and microtubules that causes transitions and fluctuations of microtubules between coherent and incoherent states. Microtubules are photon conductors. Photon conductors emit and absorb light and twist in a spiral pattern. This means our microtubules are affected by the biophotons in plants and trees, making us feel more relaxed. There is a biological process at play.[xx]

Once we understand how to draw energy, we can learn to harvest the energy. How we process light energy within us plays a vital role in keeping our light shining. When I go shopping in person, such as going to the farmers market, I let the food call me through its vibration and frequency. Online shopping doesn't work for me since I use my intuition and feelings to attract the right kind of experience that can enhance my health and well-being. The food we eat, the water we drink, the air we inhale and exhale, and our thoughts all feed our minds. How we process light affects how we feel and look. Thus, as humans, we need water and light to grow, just like flowers.

Biophotons are non-thermal in origin, and the emission that comes from biophotons is technically a type of bioluminescence that plays a crucial role in communicating, coordinating, and stimulating biochemical processes within our entire body. Biophotons are used by plants for quantum communication. Communication and control are two required activities (within and between cells) to maintain homeostasis. Homeostasis maintains optimal conditions for enzyme action throughout the body, as well as all cell functions. In the human body, these include the control of blood glucose concentration. If homeostasis is disrupted, it must be controlled, or a disease or disorder may result. This means our health depends on how much light we process.

How to Enhance Light?

There are ways to enhance our light through energetic healing. An example is the Life Activation process, a 3,000-year-old technique that can become a source of healing for all of us. This healing was directly brought from the King Solomon lineage and can activate codons in our DNA to carry more light. This affects our DNA to the extent that it enhances our immune system through the process of making the necessary proteins our body needs to be healthy. The Life Activation is a 22-strand DNA activation that awakens your divine blueprint and heightens your connection with your higher self. Becoming a Life Activation practitioner has allowed me to create this DNA activation while serving myself and others.

The second way to enhance our light is through the ancient teaching of Kabbalah, which sheds light on how light affects us in all our existence. This primal light source is funneled to our human body by our crown chakra, which sits on top of our skull. It gets distributed to our body following the Tree of Life pattern. Chakra in Sanskrit means "wheel" and refers to energy points in our body. Chakras are spinning disks of energy that perform optimally when open and aligned. Chakras correspond to bundles of nerves, major organs, and areas of our energetic body that affect our emotional and physical well-being.

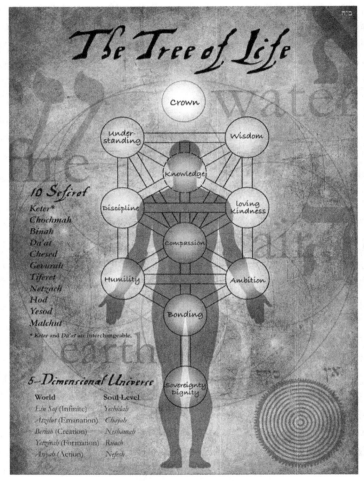

The Tree of Life is embedded in the Flower of Life
pattern and shown with Kabbalah symbology

The Kabbalah is a study of the Tree of Life embedded within the Flower of Life pattern. The Tree of Life is a graphic symbology showing the creation process with a practical roadmap for our path of spiritual growth. The Tree of Life pattern depicts the map of consciousness. This map and its path explain our spiritual origins and give us a working model for the path of return to that origination point through Sephiroth. Sephiroth means emanations, or powers, by which God the Creator is manifested. Wisdom from the Tree of Life goes all the way back to the Sumerians. Tree of Life wisdom is embedded in Kabbalah teaching.

The practice of mysticism provides knowledge to comprehend the Tree of Life, and our continued implementation of this knowledge brings transformation through Magick into our daily life via heartfelt manifestation. We can further enhance our light by understanding how time plays a role because light is interwoven with time.

Light is Interwoven with Time

Our very existence is affected by our position with the Earth, Moon, and the Central Sun. From moment to moment, our consciousness level is affected by time and the space we occupy. Per Vedic astrology that goes back 50,000 years, time and space directly affect human evolution. The planet is rotating. In a few hours, we call it midnight. In a few more hours, we call it a day. Then, we call it midnight again. Since the Earth orbits the Sun and rotates on its axis simultaneously, the Moon moves around Earth, causing us to experience seasons, day and night, changing shadows throughout the day.

Vedic defines the movement of the planet over a period of time as "yuga." Earth's position within a yuga time frame affects the etheric content in the atmosphere. These etheric contents, also known as aether, are affected by the position of the sunlight. So, based on our position within a yuga, we are affected by how much light we receive and emit and how much human potential we can exude.

Our human emotions are connected to the Moon. For example, based on the position of the Moon with respect to Earth, ocean tides are affected, and our moods are affected, hence the term "lunatics." (Luna is the Latin term for moon.)

Human perception is affected by our position from the Sun because of how we process light. Stepping into the light refers to getting out of your own way by realizing your role in the bigger scheme of things.

The universe synchronizes everything beautifully; we just have to tune into our higher self and get out of our own way. One method we can use to do this is understanding what we fear. Why are we not stepping forward? What is holding us back?

Walter Russell explains,

> *"We have infinite reference frames within our universe because light has momentum, and momentum is frame dependent. Each object or observer will have its own reference frame with its own future uncertainty as time unfolds photon by photon; therefore, an observer can look back in time at the beauty of stars in all directions from the center of their own reference frame. This is because they are forming their own space-time by collapsing the waves of light into new photon oscillations, forming their own future potential. An artist will take energy and time to create the work of art because atoms of hand and eye have bonded together, forming the movement of electric charge creating his/her own potential future. Creation is truly in the hand and eye of the beholder."*

What Walter Russell is saying is that *we* are the universe affecting ourselves continually since everything is in motion at all times. This is the circle of life. If our eyes are more sensitive to the different wavelengths of light, we would realize that everything radiates electromagnetic light waves continuously. This forms a great dance of energy exchange through a process of spontaneous and continuous changes—the aging process within the flow of time.

When we stay aligned within ourselves, when all aspects of ourselves are in harmony and functioning well, our aura enhances because of the increased light within us.

Aura Enhances Light

When we are in the presence of another person, plant, crystal, or some sort of nature, we are actually touching our invisible electromagnetic fields. This leads to changing the course of action for all the parties involved. Hindu religion uses "namaste" as a greeting to qualify our interactions, similar to praying over food before consuming it. The spiritual meaning of namaste, a Sanskrit word, is to acknowledge the light within each of us. This refers to connecting to the divine spirit or light in each person we meet and honoring them.

Our human body emits energy, extending all around the physical body like an energy shield covering and protecting all of the body. These energies are comprised of multiple interconnected layers of electromagnetic energy fields referred to as auras. An aura is another example of a system of intricate patterns that creates the entire framework through which our awareness of life unfolds. These patterns are located in an area of about 55 feet in diameter that surrounds our body.

Unique, artistic renderings of our invisible aura—
an energy shield surrounding our human body

The human energy field or aura body projects our consciousness through a holographic template that generates the physical manifestations we experience within this material Reality. *"Our aura is literally broadcasting God's energy all over the cosmos, and people who get in tune will be affected by it —the human aura."* This means we are emitting an electromagnetic field that is affecting others at all times, whether one is tuned to it or not.

The auric field contains every aspect of our life from the very beginning until this moment, right now. It includes the record of every personality pattern, experience, desire, belief, thought, and event — everything! As our aura enhances, we become stronger as quantum beings and are more protected from external challenges.

Activating Merkabah is another way for us to enhance our auras. Merkabah translates literally to light (Mer), spirit (Ka), and body (bah). The Merkabah symbol is a shape made of two intersecting tetrahedrons that spin in opposite directions, creating a three-dimensional energy field. The opposite direction represents masculine energy. The feminine energy represents consciousness energy that spirals to generate a DNA and RNA imprint. The DNA architecture is the masculine principle, while the RNA is the feminine principle.

When we activate Merkabah via aligning with the Sun, every cell in our quantum being releases a photon of light. This release affects our blood and crystalline matrices within, and the next stage of evolution gets unlocked. Hence, Merkabah is a dimensional elevator that amplifies our manifestation. The reason for this amplification of aura is due to the increased bandwidth in our capacity to receive and transmit information with everything around us. We must learn to harness this photonic energy to expedite our evolutionary process. The Merkabah fields can help us sustain the energy by building the entire light body construct.

Albert Einstein articulated,

> *"We have slowed down sound and light waves, a walking bundle of frequencies tuned into the cos-*

mos. We are souls dressed up in sacred biochemical garments, and our bodies are the instruments through which our souls play their music. We can see the soul of a person through their eyes because light shines through their eyes."

Within our light body, our individual choice of expressing emotion, thought, memory, and experience all contribute to the manifestation of knowledge and form into physical matter.

The Great Central Sun, different from the Sun that shines upon us, serves as a portal from the material realm to the spiritual. William Herschel (1738-1822) and Johann Heinrich von Mädler (1794-1874), who came up with the Central Sun hypothesis, suggested that the center of the galaxy was located in the Pleiades star cluster, around which the Sun revolves. We are transmitting and receiving moment to moment as a crystalline, quantum being. These effects are created by the absorption and emission of photons in our light bodies. We are affecting each other at the micro level and influenced by the Sun at the macro level.

We can play a piece of beautiful music when we are in tune with our light within. We can also create powerful Magickal experiences for ourselves and others.

Stepping into your light is the key to igniting yourself as a quantum human craft. It is also the key to unveiling the Magickal world all around us. When we enhance the light within us, we affect our manifestations via tapping into our quantum power. This is the secret to conscious living and experiencing. This is how we gain a greater range of joy and fulfillment within the unlimited possibilities of co-creation. Stars are born through an alchemical process. You are a Star. Keep shining your light!

∏ctivating the Merkabah:

How can you enhance your light and your aura so that you manifest a more positive experience for yourself?

1. First, clear your mind, sit down, and relax.

   ➤ Visualize your Merkabah and allow the male pyramid to point upward and the female to point downward.
   ➤ Make it spin so that it begins to activate. Spin the male pyramid from left to right around your body (CW) and do the opposite (ACW) for the female pyramid. Per Barbara Marciniak, move 33 times in the clockwise direction to accelerate your enlightenment.

Start doing it once a day, and you will see how your Reality starts to change.

Live Life

Let us Live and Be in the Flow!
Starting from scratch again is hard,
But still, the choice is yours.

If you feel stuck,
Then make a different choice this time.
Because if you don't,
Not making a choice is still a choice.

Life is to live, learn, and evolve;
If you stay stuck, you don't even live.

And when you don't live,
You affect others whom you love.

Because we are all interconnected,
Everything we do and don't do
Ultimately affects ourselves and others.

So free yourself and go live
Life is too short not to!

Scan the code above with you smart phone to view
a message from Shehnaz – or follow this link:

https://youtu.be/Sl4mZbw4ogw

Chapter 10

Quantum Universe

Observation affects the momentum.
-Shehnaz Soni

W e are human beings who live in a perpetual existence within the quantum universe. Being human, we are conduits in how we create our daily experiences via interaction. These interactions can be mere observation or focused attention. Where thought goes, energy flows, and that dance between us and the quantum universe makes us go through a live, stimulating storyline in a game called life. The more we understand our participation in our universe, the better off we are.

What are we made of at the fundamental level? What is the smallest particle we are made of? Scientific research is continually evolving our understanding. Based on our current knowledge, the human body can be broken down into cells, molecules, and clusters of atoms. Atoms can be further broken down into electrons revolving around their orbit, just like a solar system, with protons and neutrons representing the Sun. To date, quarks and leptons are designated as fundamental particles making up all the ordinary matter we know.

What does an Atom consist of?

CERN, Council of European Nuclear Research, founded in 1954, is spending all its energy on understanding what we are made of at the fundamental level using the Large Hadron Collider (LHC). The LHC is the most powerful particle accelerator in the world. These particles are accelerated to a speed close to that of light. So they collide to recreate the same scenario the universe encountered in its origination during the Big Bang. In the process, we are interfering since these collisions produce particles, such as the Higgs boson or the exotic particles we recently discovered. These discoveries are affecting the universe as we know it.

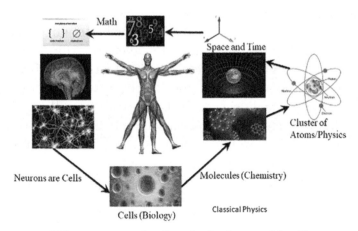

What are we made of at the fundamental level?

The following figure shows the human body is made of cells, cells are composed of molecules, molecules are composed of atoms, and atoms are composed of electrons, protons, and neutrons. Electron particles occupy space and time and sit in a set of coordinates (X, Y, Z, TIME). These coordinates represent our existence in this physical dimension. This set of coordinates can be determined by math. Math is considered a universal language by scholars and scientists. It is a tool invented by a scientist like Isaac Newton to understand the concepts of physics. If we can explain quantum physics via math, maybe we can understand ourselves better.

In a nutshell, quantum physics explains that matter is not made up of particles but waves. That means everything we see, hear, touch, taste, or smell is, in Reality, a wave of information and energy.

Quantum physics can be explained by the following example:

When we notice someone looking at us, we sense it and instantaneously look at them. They look away. Why? Because they sensed us as well.

The best way to explain the quantum nature of our universe is via the double-slit experiment that shows an electron exists in particle form in one scenario and waveform in another. The double-slit experiment is explained below with the setup, explanation, and outcome.

Double-Slit Experiment

Setup:

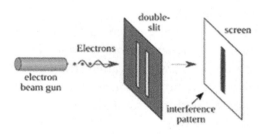

Double-Slit Experiment Setup

Explanation:

In quantum mechanics, the double-slit experiment demonstrates the inseparability of the wave and particle natures of light and other quantum particles.

An electron is emitted from the electron beam gun to pass through the two slits. We see a different response from the electron based on whether we look at this experiment while it's occurring.

Outcome:

1. Electrons depict wave-like characteristics when we don't observe an atom.
    ➢ The electron goes through each slit, both slits and neither slit simultaneously.
    ➢ Electrons exist in a quantum superposition; every possible outcome exists at the same time.
2. Electrons depict particle-like characteristics when we spy on the atom.

Murphy's law, which states that anything that can go wrong will go wrong, can be explained by the quantum nature of the universe. For example, the Double-Slit-Experiment has already proved the effect of observation on an electron. Observation affects the momentum. Numerous research studies have shown that atoms won't change when they are being watched, similar to the adage that "a watched pot never boils" since observing a wave function causes the superposition to collapse. Superposition is the ability of a quantum system to be in multiple states at the same time until it is measured.

The word reconnaissance is used in the military world for observation. When we perform reconnaissance on an enemy, no matter how discrete we are, we still affect the outcome and what comes next regarding our interaction with the enemy.

When we desire something, we add expectation to the equation on top of observation, affecting the overall outcome and experience even more. Have you heard of couples who try to conceive babies and don't succeed? Often, these couples end up adopting a child and a few months later become pregnant. This is the effect of expectation on what we want to manifest. Therefore, we have to be conscious of our actions at all times.

> *Observation creates a quantum collapse to a timeline.*
> *Choose to observe wisely.*

Dr. Stuart explains superposition and how it collapses on observation,

> *"Things can be in multiple places or act like waves, kind of smeared out as probabilities, rather than being definite particles with specific locations and trajectories. And some quantum physicists say that until a quantum system is consciously observed or measured, it remains in a superposition of multiple possibilities, multiple coexisting states. But once measured, the quantum probability wave instantly collapses or reduces to just one state."*[xxi]

This understanding gives birth to two schools of thought:
1. Does Reality exist around us even if we are not observing?
2. Does Reality only exist when we observe?

Both understandings can have dynamic effects on our Reality and what Reality is. The results of this double-slit experiment clearly tell us that the observer's consciousness is required to bring the universe into existence. The observer's consciousness is affected by their belief, free will, and intentions. For example, when we take a picture from a camera, we freeze the moving frame of electrons.

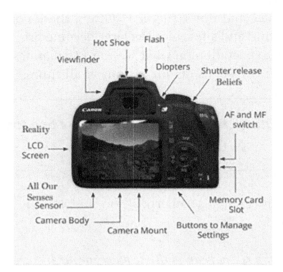

Camera depicting example for the quantum collapse

The act of observing creates a quantum entanglement and quantum collapse. When we experience something by ourselves that is marvelous, we want to tell a friend about this experience and take them with us so they can encounter the same thing. Do they experience what we wanted to share in the first place? Probably not because we have added expectation and a friend as a variable in the equation. This new experience is not relatable at all. What just happened? Quantum entanglement, quantum physics, and quantum collapse.

For example, when I would play the video game "Empire Earth," I would notice the world would light up as I traveled along the path and my computer mouse allowed me to explore new vistas. Is it the same in our life? If yes, shouldn't we be observing and exploring paths that are exciting and appeal to our curiosity?

We have free will. With all the information we process every nanosecond, I wonder how much free will we truly exercise every day? Isn't free will the freedom of humans to make choices that are not determined by prior causes or divine intervention? This free will exemplifies how quantum collapse differs with each variation in every scenario. Quantum collapse is what solidifies Reality for us.

Who instigate the quantum collapse – consciousness versus observation?

Is it a quantum collapse that gives off conscious awareness, or is it the other way around? Let's take a quick look at both of these theories. Contrary to the first – Reality exists around us even if we are not observing, and in favor of the second – Reality only exists when we observe. Niels Bohr's Copenhagen interpretation states that anything unobserved would be in a wave-like state of quantum superposition. However, Sir Roger Penrose, professor of math at the University of Oxford and one of Stephen Hawking's mentors, provides an alternative to Copenhagen's interpretation in favor of asking the question, *"What about quantum activity inside a human brain?"* So, the chicken or egg, which comes first, is the question.

Roger proposed that in such cases, once the wave function proceeds to a certain point, it self-collapses due to an intrinsic, objective threshold in the fabric of spacetime itself. When the collapse of that superposition happens, a moment of consciousness occurs. In other words, Roger argued that consciousness doesn't cause the quantum wave-function collapse, as the Copenhagen interpretation says. Rather, Roger suggested that consciousness *is* the wave function collapse or at least one particular kind of collapse.

John Wheeler says observation is the action of a conscious mind and, *"We are part of a universe that is a work in progress. We are tiny patches of the universe looking at itself and the building of itself. We live in a participatory world."*

Participatory Universe

Dr. Robert Lanza, who was part of the team that cloned the world's first early-stage human embryos, describes reality as a process that fundamentally involves consciousness. He explains how, without consciousness, all matter dwells in an undetermined state of probability. This theory was a wake-up call and was seconded by David, an astrophysicist at NASA.[xxii]

If we live in a participatory world, as John Wheeler suggested, many factors are attributed to our level of consciousness. This affects our laws of attraction and vibration.

Do we live in a Participatory Universe?

It's important to understand our quantum beingness (uniqueness) and our interface with everything that surrounds us.

> ➤ Belief and thought directly result from the story we tell ourselves consciously and subconsciously. We are pulling in data streams all the time based on our thoughts and beliefs. If we've had a track record of unhappy endings, we may keep tapping into the same negative data stream, repeating the patterns that then cause us to give up on our dreams.

➤ Known unknowns are the ones we are consciously aware of. We understand that drinking more than one cup of coffee a day may affect our bodies negatively, but we don't perceive the problem as worrisome enough to take action. For example, drugs induce a biochemical and electromagnetic reaction within the mind heightening many things that cause both beneficial and adverse effects.

➤ Consensus Reality is agreed-upon beliefs or concepts of Reality that people in the world, a culture, or a group, believe are Real (or treated as Real). This is usually based on their shared experiences. We all agree that a particular object is a table, or a candle, based on agreements we have all made with each other. The Consensus Reality created is based on the majority of human consensus without an individual's unique perceptions.

> *Even though we live in a somewhat predestined world, well-choreographed by all the inputs and outputs, we still live in an indeterministic world due to unknown unknowns combined with our subconscious programming.*

Unknown unknowns are things we do to ourselves without realizing it. For example, sometimes, we get into a toxic relationship and still don't do anything about it since we haven't given ourselves permission to be happy. These self-sabotaging behaviors stem from our subconscious programming.

We have heard before that our beliefs and thoughts affect our biology and biography. For example, with beliefs, if I believe that I can't live alone, then all decisions I make in life stem from not being able to live alone. I will tolerate the codependent relationship because of the fear of being alone. This fear will affect my health and biology. This belief will also keep me where I am in life affecting my biography.

Let us use the following example of affecting your biology. Try this; pay attention to your breathing for a moment. Breathe four-fold breaths (breathe in 4, hold 4, breathe out 4, hold 4) and observe your thoughts as you breathe. What happened? Your thoughts were distracted because you were focused on breathing, weren't they? Let's say you noticed while breathing that your nose felt a little dry. What happens now? Your attention moves on to the dry nose. It is spring, and pollen is everywhere. If you believe in allergies making your nose dry, you will justify your belief, and then you might reinforce it by saying it back to yourself. Your thoughts and breathing are intertwined and affect your body at the cellular level.

I love my life now more than ever. It's because my perspective has changed. When you look at Adam and Eve's story, one can think of getting out of Heaven as a terrible thing for their future. What if I say that Adam and Eve didn't leave Eden physically? It is their perspective that changed and caused all this havoc. It's something to ponder as we try to understand how we co-create our reality based on our beliefs and perception.

Does objective Reality exist in a true sense? Or is consciousness experiencing itself fractally? If Reality had any sort of existence, it would look like an endless sea of static information in which all probabilities exist, similar to the image shown in the movie *The Matrix*.

Also, in the movie *Contact*, Jodie Foster returns from her outer space travel. Jodie Foster plays the role of an astronaut who works for the Search for Extraterrestrial Intelligence (SETI) program hoping to find evidence of alien life. During this travel, she experienced meeting an extra-terrestrial, who showed up looking and sounding like her father when he was alive. When she shares this experience back on Earth, it is not comprehended by others. Everyone denies her credibility. Why? Because others didn't experience what Jodie experienced. Due to her travel being outside of the physical realm and beyond our limited comprehension, people could not understand. Later, the movie shows a static recording of the entire experience, proving her unexplainable experience.

Every moment of experience is a Reality in itself. We can affect our outcome with a slight variation in our intention and the underlying belief we hold onto to create our desired manifestation. Minuscule change is compounded over time, just like a drop of water making an ocean over time.

In a chess game, you want to be 20 steps ahead to win the game. We have to do the same to create Heaven on Earth. We must know what those steps are and take them one by one, like Jacob's ladder. Jacob's ladder is the ladder of the created universe. It appeared in a dream to Jacob, who saw it stretching from Heaven to Earth, with angels going up and down the ladder one step at a time.

The universe branches whenever a quantum system superimposes or entangles its environment. However, we perceive this Reality only when our wave function collapses via the quantum collapse phenomenon. Quantum entanglement is an inevitable feature of Reality that affects our day-to-day manifestation.

Quantum Entanglement

Quantum entanglement is a physical phenomenon that occurs when pairs or groups of particles, such as photons, are generated, interact, or share spatial proximity. This phenomenon occurs in such a way that the quantum state of each particle can't be described independently without the state of the others, even when the particles are separated by a considerable distance.

Let's say we have a particle A and a particle B. When particles are quantumly entangled, particle A can react before particle B is physically stimulated. Albert Einstein called quantum entanglement "spooky action at a distance."

Quantumly entangled particles create an energetically strong bond; therefore, the effects are everlasting. Quantum entanglement is stronger between particles that are emotionally attached versus ones that are not. This means particles of thought can entangle with another person's thought particles via an extra-sensory perception (ESP). In real life, we see quantum entanglement among couples who love each other very deeply. The bond of love is so powerful that it affects every aspect of beingness. You aren't in control of your body, thoughts, etc. You are positively compromised! We make Vesica Pisces when we form an unbreakable bond.

In a quantum model, all of existence is encoded in a quantized moment of consciousness that contains all of our experiences. Quantum physics suggests that energy comes in discrete units called quanta. Quanta of consciousness come in a spectrum of different intensities, frequencies, and qualities.

If we can entangle with other particles, can we entangle with the dark matter of the universe where vast information resides, like Akashic records? When psychics offer an Akashi reading or fortune telling of any kind, where do you think they are tapping into to get the information? They are tapping into the morphogenetic field available to all of us.

For example, vibration from crystal makes waves that human receptors pick up and convert back to binary information. That is why crystals are used for fortune telling under King Solomon's mystical teachings. For example, most of the Great Pyramid structures are made of granite, a quartz crystal. Since a quartz crystal can be perfectly tuned to the human mind when we are in an altered state of consciousness. This is why shamans use quartz crystals to connect with God.

When crystal comes into contact with humans, a transfer of data occurs. The king's chamber in the Great Pyramid is encased in granite. Jacob's ladder to the seven levels of Heaven was only envisaged once Jacob laid his head upon a granite stone slab. Similarly, Adepts, the great Hindu and Buddhist Tantric practitioners of medieval India, use mandalas to see hidden messages only retrieved by the third eye when the mind resonates at the same frequency as quartz crystal.

Quantum coherence occurs when we are in nature and refers to the ability of a quantum state to maintain its entanglement and superposition in the face of interactions and thermalization. If we entangle with nature, we can connect with God, the mind of all. We heal ourselves naturally.

Quantum wave function is when all possible outcomes collapse into one specific outcome. That is how we quantum manifest. We can leverage the understanding of quantum entanglement, which means choosing with whom and with what we entangle to affect our daily manifestation as quantum beings.

The Quantum Manifestation

Manifestation is the embodiment of an abstract idea that is not in your Reality yet. The quantum manifestation is your state in between, from unmanifest to manifest, a bridge that links you to a new Reality, a new version of you. Quantum physics proves that when we interact with the world and form quantum entanglement, we take a quantum jump or leap into a new Reality. This is the key to quantum manifestation.

Quantum jumping is the process by which a person envisions a desired result or state of being that differs from the existing situation. The person also observes that possibility by supplying sufficient energy to leap into that alternate Reality. For example, you can turn on your favorite empowering music, listen, dance, and get lost in the world of imagination.

Quantum jumping is how we traverse time, space, and matter:

➢ We traverse time by losing awareness of it.
➢ We traverse space by not being attached to our position on Earth.
➢ We traverse matter via reprogramming of our DNA at the subconscious level.

To maintain the new Reality, you have to comprehend how our individual choices of expressing emotion, thought, memory, and experience play a role. So, you can create a plan for your daily routine.

Why are we not teaching our younger generation the very concept that makes our life exciting and liberating? More than 100 years ago, we established the understanding of the quantum nature of our existence, and yet, we are still not teaching our younger generation.

Everyone is unique and has specific gifts to offer to affect the mass consciousness. Schools teach students societal norms and a standard way of thinking that does not advocate for uniqueness and creativity. Schools don't teach students how to manage their minds to create a Reality that is better suited for them.

My son uses his left hemisphere reasoning when adopting new concepts. He recently asked me how to discern between waves and particles in terms of manifestation. This is how I responded to him:

> Consciousness enables a quantum collapse from a wave (unmanifested=0) to a particle (manifested=1).
> A wave is represented as zero-point energy, where all possibilities exist like untapped potential.
> A particle is represented in our physical dimension as a dense object.

Every dimension affects another due to photons being in contact with each other.

Dimensions are a spacetime operating framework creating a fundamental for the perception we operate from.

Based on M theory which encompasses string theory, we have 11 dimensions. The 11th dimension is a characteristic of spacetime that has been proposed as a possible answer to questions that arise in Superstring Theory. Superstring Theory states the existence of nine dimensions of space and one dimension of time. Dimensions are 90 degrees from each other.

Higher dimensions can explain lower dimensions. For example, if we are holding a 3-dimensional cube in our hand, the shadow is a 2-dimensional cube on the ground. Only the person holding the 3-dimensional cube can have a larger perspective of what the cube consists of beyond 2D. This is a key to understanding dimensions.

You can't understand the 4D Reality by living in a 3D Reality. You need to understand 4D Reality by experiencing it yourself. If you are in a 2-dimensional operating space, you can't even comprehend 3D; however, you can imagine.

> *We transcend dimensions beyond*
> *space-time via imagination.*

For example, you want to buy a new car. The car exists as a possibility in the form of a **wave** in the quantum universe. Using your **consciousness**, you can focus on a car of your choosing, and it will ultimately be in your manifestation. This understanding is the key to manifestation.

Growing up as a devout Muslim, I prayed five times a day. I was a pious, obedient Muslim girl, striving to be the perfect Muslim. My piousness was the direct result of my consciousness and how I saw and felt the world around me. I was sensitive to my surroundings and felt everything very deeply. I had a strong desire to be respected by society; therefore, I dreamed of becoming fluent in English because society respected those who spoke English. My consciousness and desire to become one with manifesting fluency in the English language was very farfetched for someone like me. This was because I attended Urdu schools growing up and had no experience with speaking the English language.

Today, I speak English daily to convey spiritual concepts to a room full of ministers and leaders or communicate the reliability of ballistic missiles to the higher echelon in the military. I didn't give up on my dream. I prayed and imagined speaking English. Even though I had no idea how I would manifest it. I still follow quantum manifestation steps, believing in my dreams and taking action every day.

Binary World

Life is eternal and follows an intelligent, self-organizing, self-regulating principle. In a quantum world, we have infinite possibilities between "zero" and "one." What makes us look for changes in our life? What makes state transfer from zero to one and back and forth? Inner fire is the answer. Passion is the answer. We can't sleep until we do what we are born to do. That is how we "move the mountain," and a change of state occurs.

The fire burning within us to expand our consciousness creates a trigger. Life decides to have a different experience, and a new "thoughtform" emerges. These thoughtforms are energy blueprints. Rearranging occurs in our patterns and "state changes" due to the intention of creating new experiences. This state change causes the movement in our energy field, photons get released, and a new form gets created. This quantum process is how we change our Reality and manifest at the quantum level.

The *Matrix* movie depicts the green screen showing bits 0 and 1 in a vertical formation, scrolling up and down like a vibration. This is because every process in the universe can be reduced to interactions between particles that produce binary answers: yes or no, here or there, up or down, light or dark. In mathematics and digital electronics, a binary number is a number expressed in the base-2 numeral system or binary numeral system. This system uses only two **symbols: typically, "0" and "1." Therefore, everything in our existence** narrows down to bits 0 and 1—all or nothing.

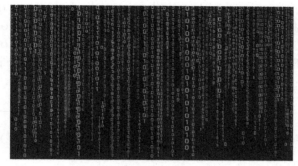

This screen depicts machine language – a collection of binary bits

Another way to explain our binary existence is through "Hold and Release." Our muscles contract and expand. Every moment we are deciding what to hold on to and what to let go of to create a Reality of our choosing. We are holding on to and releasing at all times. This action is performed at the minuscule level. For example, it can include what clothes to hold on to and which to let go of. It can apply to which relationships we hold on to and let go of.

> *By choosing, we tune in to the ongoing music within our DNA and traverse time and space to become magnificent surfers.*

In the movie, the *Matrix* is an illusion that has enslaved humanity. We have the power to break away from dangerous illusions, but we have to make a conscious choice to do so, just like the characters in the movie. In The *Matrix*, the blue pill allows the subject to remain in the fabricated Reality of the Matrix; the red pill serves as a "location device" to find the subject's body in the Real world and to prepare them to be "unplugged" from the Matrix. Once one chooses the red or blue pill, the choice is irrevocable.

Every single yes and no brings diverse experiences. Every time we say yes to something, we are saying no to something else.

So, we are choosing a side whether we acknowledge it or not. As a natural-born leader, I had inner knowing not to let other peoples' "No" be my "No." I said "Yes" to myself when "No" was the response from the majority. This wasn't easy. However, it was the best route for my Magickal life.

> ### *Leadership is not an ability, but a responsibility.*

What initiates us towards a discrete yes? How can you stand up for yourself if you are the only one standing? You should pick the option that resonates the most with you in each moment. It is hard, but not impossible. Once you stand true to yourself, others might stand up right beside you.

When we observe cell creation during the early development of a human baby, we can see the correlation between human cells and binary systems. Correlation is a mutual relationship or connection between two or more things.

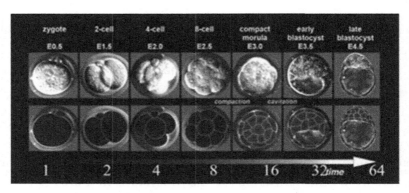

Notice the patterns that emerge as the cells of a human baby develop

When we apply the numerology here, we get numbers 1, 2, 4, 8, 7, 5, 1, and then the pattern keeps repeating. Three numbers are missing from this pattern; 3, 6, and 9. Where are they? They are hidden inside the vortex, Tube Torus, our non-physical auric fields. Vortex-based mathematics is the best way to understand how energy expresses itself mathematically. This type of math shows the dimensional shape and function of the universe as a toroid or doughnut-shaped black hole. In vortex math, if you polarize everything, the numbers 1, 2, 4, 5, 7, and 8 are numbers that represent the physical world. The numbers 3, 6, and 9 represent the spiritual and non-physical world.

The spiritual world governs the physical world from the quantum level. The numbers 3, 6, and 9 are the "Tesla Code." Per Tesla, *"If you only knew the magnificence of the 3, 6, and 9, then you would have the key to the universe."*

We live in a binary world physically. It is depicted in the Flower of Life pattern. It is defined in cell creation during the early development of a human baby. 3, 6, and 9 numbers are missing from the binary world. Meaning there is a possible quantum wave unmanifested, hidden inside the morphogenetic field of our aura. While binary numbers represent what evolves physically, the Tesla code hides what we can't see in the form of zero-point energy. Everything we know incorporates this understanding. That is where the secret of manifestation lies.

> *Binary number (physical) + Tesla code (nonphysical)*
> *= the Quantum Universe.*

The Phi/Fibonacci sequence represents how things evolve fractally, encompassing all physical and nonphysical attributes.

The quantum universe is intelligent at the subatomic level and acts as a DNA feedback loop. DNA sends up purposeful signals in order to grow, and it waits for a signal to come back before proceeding.

Quantum physics helps us realize how powerful our consciousness is and can affect our daily lives if we tune into it more deliberately. Our consciousness keeps evolving via our minds as we observe our surroundings 24 hours a day.

> *The quantum universe opens the door to*
> *infinite possibilities for our future.*

It opens the door to the type of Reality we would like to collapse from moment to moment. It opens the door to bringing in desired experiences in our daily life.

It opens the door to using our innate ability to keep our attention focused on our consciousness, thoughts, beliefs, and triggers to manifest our dream life.

Quantum Manifestation

1. What gets you excited to live each day?
2. What is your heart's true desire?

   - All the money you want.
   - No responsibility, obligations, or expectations.
   - No fear, guilt, regrets, or past triggers.

3. What keeps you awake at night?
4. Whatever your answer is to questions 1, 2, and 3, let us make that your Reality.
5. What minuscule action can you take today to get closer to experiencing this dream?
6. Make a plan to add this action to your calendar.
7. Give yourself a pat on your back as you take action daily.
8. See the Magick unfold right before your eyes.

Manifestation Process

The Circle of Creation

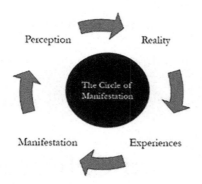

369 Implementation

There are various techniques to avail the 3, 6, 9, Tesla code in our daily lives to enhance our manifesting experience.

I use numbers to guide me in making decisions. It can come in the form of an address, dates to fly, or even the number of times one might perform an activity.

You can plan important milestones in your life using 369 methods. For example, I fly on numerology 3, return on numerology 9 and stay for 6 days during my travel.

Affirmation- DNA Upgrade

We can upgrade our DNA by indulging in an activity that can reprogram our subconscious.

1. Write three affirmations based on your manifestation goals.
2. Repeat them three times a day for 21 days.

This will activate Tesla code 369 and help you upgrade your DNA and life.

State of Coherence

Coherence is created by changing the frequency and amplitude of the electrostatic field. This is accomplished in the human mind by determining the configuration of the holographic energy matrix. *"Coherence is the state when the heart, mind, and emotions are in energetic alignment and cooperation,"* says HeartMath Institute Research Director Dr. Rollin McCraty.

Individual level:

1. Create the state of coherence in your daily life:
   The state of coherence can be created by meditation, being in nature rituals, daily affirmation calls, or unique spiritual traits.

Group level:

2. Create the state of coherence in your group collaboration activities: The state of coherence can be created by group meditation, spiritual exercises, etc.

Make it a priority to stay in a state of coherence.

Continue to do steps 1 and 2, and your world will run on coherence continuously.

Scan the code above with you smart phone to view
a message from Shehnaz – or follow this link:

https://youtu.be/6Iq5rKRo-OA

Chapter 11

Conscious Evolution

Conscious Evolution happens when
we experience a state of bliss.
—Shehnaz Soni

*W*e are here to gain experiences, evolve, and start a brand-new journey each day. Every day the Sun comes up. Every day offers a new opportunity to do something grand because it may be our last day. So, what is the reason for learning these lessons and storing them in our memory in the form of beliefs and thoughts? There is a "ladder logic" at work. We take steps in our life to continue on to the next level as we evolve in this life form.

We experience life in the form of Reality. Reality is what we perceive as truth based on our consciousness level and our awareness of it. Awareness is knowledge or perception of a situation or fact.

Wherever you are in life, awareness is your first step to influencing your patterns and your life. Awareness enables us to fix our day-to-day life challenges with a new acceptable pattern in our first step toward change. This key message empowers you to start making deep and lasting shifts in your life as you create your Heaven on Earth. In every state of my life, when I made an important decision and a drastic change, the first trigger was *awareness* of the challenge.

> ## The underlying pattern of our consciousness defines our entire Reality.

Therefore, consciousness is the driving force that helps us transcend or move through the universe. We, as humans, transcend by moving energy through learning, growing, and evolving. We are always going forward since we process our Reality linearly. Per my colleague and friend, Elizabeth April, *"A universe is a collection of atomic and subatomic particles navigated through the vibration of consciousness."* The physical world is described by atomic and subatomic particles moving through energy.

Our inner child is always on a quest for truth, understanding, and contentment. We should ask ourselves these simple but thought-provoking questions:

1. Who am I?
2. What am I?
3. Where do I come from?
4. Where am I going?
5. What is my purpose?
6. Why am I here?
7. What is here?
8. When does it all end?
9. Does it ever end?

We can get lost in these questions, but don't let that discourage you. We find ourselves only after being lost. These questions help us discover the root cause of our existence as quantum beings.

In order to answer these questions, let us go to the basics.

What is the mind, and how does it differ from our consciousness? If the mind is the platform through which the program called "life" runs, then the mind is an operating system (OS). An OS contains software that manages the computer's hardware and software as well as all of its memory, processes, and communications. The mind functions as the OS for humans. Consciousness is the software through which an individual feels, perceives, thinks, and reasons. For example, if our finger touches a burning flame, we feel the burn and scream despite potentially embarrassing ourselves in front of others. We are experiencing the outcome of the delicate processing of the mind through consciousness.

Consciousness is awareness of our existence; self-awareness is recognition of that awareness. Therefore, humans are more than just conscious; they are self-aware. Awareness can be represented by the amount of light needed to make an object visible. Awareness can be a flashlight or a flood light, depending on your level of consciousness. In computer terms, awareness is the application that runs based on focused attention.

Where does self-awareness come from? Dr. David Rudrauf, a renowned researcher in the field of self-awareness, discovered that *"self-awareness cannot be localized to a single region of the brain."* His team used a multidisciplinary approach for the study, combining virtual Reality, neuroimaging, computational modeling, and robotics. In this study, a 57-year-old, college-educated man known as Patient R, with a severely damaged brain, passed all standard self-awareness tests. He displayed repeated self-recognition, both when looking in the mirror and identifying himself in unaltered photographs taken during all periods of his life. Patient R is missing all the areas in the brain that are typically thought to be needed for self-awareness. Yet, he remains self-aware."[xxiii]

> *By being aware, we are conscious,*
> *and by being conscious, we are self-aware.*

This biofeedback loop between consciousness and self-awareness keeps us in the ever-expanding cycle of conscious living.

Biofeedback is a process by which electronic monitoring of a normally automatic bodily function is used to train someone to acquire voluntary control of that function. This voluntary control is obtained through reinforcing this behavior.

As soon as we are born, we experience life. We experience life via perceiving Reality. In short, consciousness creates our Reality, not the matter! The matter is 99% space. Therefore, Professor of Philosophy David Chalmers states, *"How does something as immaterial as consciousness arise from something as unconscious as matter?"* We can simplify this by asking how consciousness manifests into all these diverse forms. Life is not evolving; consciousness is. "Matter derives from the mind, not mind from matter," suggests the "Tibetan Book of the Great Liberation." Keep in mind that we are using consciousness and mind interchangeably here.

The unconscious world that resides in dark matter is where all our manifestations are held until they become physical. Our conscious mind divides Reality while our unconscious mind unites dreams. Real Magick is understanding the difference between dreams and Reality while using methods to control and work with both realms.

The quantum universe has demonstrated the relationship between the mind (the observer) and matter (the observed). Dr. Stuart looks at the mind and matter relationship differently. He says,

> *"There's no matter there! There's something else. I call it spacetime geometry; the Hindus call it 'Brahman.' You can call it whatever you like— spirit, the cosmos, quantum gravity—whatever it is that gives rise to both mind and matter and underlies all of Reality."*

This quote gives all the credit of Reality to what is hidden in the form of spacetime geometry.[xxiv]

Everything we experience in the physical universe exists in an ocean of infinite possibilities coming into existence when the mind working with consciousness gives it "form." Let's take a look at the following famous quote from Tesla, *"To create and to annihilate material substance, cause it to aggregate in forms according to his desire, would be the supreme manifestation of the power of man's mind, his most complete triumph over the physical world."*

Peter Russell, an author of "From Science to God," also says it very well, *"There is only one consciousness. Variations in the consciousness field (form) are perceived in the mind. The material world is the appearance in the mind."* This is why the spiritualization of matter occurs when we express divine presence in every aspect of creation, particularly within ourselves. This means when we live in alignment, everything seems like Magick. Based on all the scholars quoted above, we are confirming that the universe is mental, as mentioned in the book "Kybalion." What we see with our eyes is only the tip of the iceberg. What we don't see is where truth and understanding lie.[xxv]

In order to understand our mind and consciousness at a deeper level, we have to know how quantum beings process data making the holographic universe possible.

Holographic Universe

Before the cell phone, the television was the most powerful device invented to distract humanity from its purpose. The human brain has a unique way of processing information, which is why TV has become a source of entertainment. Television or far vision (TV) is a telecommunication device that transmits moving images in color and sound. Think of TV as an electronic flick-book. TV creates moving pictures by repeatedly capturing still images and presenting these frames to your eyes so quickly that they seem to be moving. Our brain processes these frames like it's all happening behind the screen.

The number of pixels in a two-dimensional grid determines its overall resolution. A pixel on the TV screen resembles Planck length in our physical atomic world. Our brain will reassemble the dots into a meaningful image. Keep in mind this attribute of our brain when processing Reality. There is an excellent reason we are not seeing the raw truth due to how we have been programmed to perceive TV.

The word "Reality" has an origin that traces back to the French in the year 1540 and means "quality of being Real." Cambridge defines Reality *as the state of things as they are, rather than as they are imagined to be.*" Cambridge's definition is ambiguous. If you are one of those people who live in your imagination, then your imagination is your Reality, isn't it? One person's perception may differ from another. This means there is a very high possibility that one person's Reality can be another person's illusion and vice-versa. Why? Because we each have a different perspective and different angles of comprehension. Even though a hologram stores information covering various angles, we only access the angle of our choosing.

A mirror gives a different impression of our face each time we see ourselves. Why? This is because several variables are at play; angles, positions, lights, our emotional state, etc. An example of this might be two birds sitting on a wire. As you drive by, their distance and position vary. Observe this experiment while you are not driving, of course, to be safe. The evidence from these observations will prove to you that your perception varies depending on your angle, motion, and position.

Our Reality is based on perception. Perspective is a channel we watch on our "lifetime TV" based on our beliefs. Our beliefs drive the experience. When we see a burning flame picture in a magazine or a video, we feel the heat in our core because we believe the flame is hot. We experience this very well-choreographed burning feeling through many factors at play in space and time. Maybe we can leverage the understanding of the variables at play in creating the holographic universe to deeply heal and update our existing versions of Reality. The holographic nature of the universe works on the same principle as watching immersive TV.

The Human Brain is Amazing
(Watching TV – Far Sight)

1. Our brain will reassemble the pixels (2 D grid) into a meaningful image.
2. TV creates moving picture by repeatedly capturing pictures and presenting these frames to your eyes so quickly that they seem to be moving.
3. Our brain processes these frames like it's all happening behind the scenes.

The Human Mind is Amazing:
(Living in a Holographic Universe)

1. When our mind puts a laser focus on physical dimension, we create a universe by perceiving it with no separation in spite of Plank length.
2. Our mind perceives by comparison only. That is why PHI ratio relates to Logarithm in Math.
3. Our mind exists as a field surrounding the brain in a parallel universe.
4. We are a projection of the Soul.
5. This is the only way we can perceive reality within time and space.

A hologram is a projection of a living pattern of the three-dimensional grid system that follows Sacred Geometry. When superimposed using mathematics, three-dimensional holograms can be reduced to two dimensions and processed via a binary system, just like a computer. Holograms are efficient since we can store billions of bits of information in a tiny space. A hologram can encode so much detail that if we take an image of a lake, under magnification, we can see the microorganisms not visible to the naked eye. The pattern of the hologram is stored everywhere on the stored medium.

The brain collects information, processes it, and projects a hologram based on the digital bits of data it receives through the electromagnetic matrix gathered by our sensory system. The mind proceeds to compare the image with itself. This means the brain compares the image received with part of its own hologram, which constitutes memory by registering differences in the geometric form and the energy frequency the consciousness perceives. Itzhak Bentov makes a great observation, stating, *"Our whole Reality is constructed by constantly making such comparisons. Whenever we perceive something, we always perceive differences only."*

According to a declassified CIA (U.S. Central Intelligence Agency) paper on the Gateway Experience that referenced the work of Itzhak Bentov, by applying biofeedback and holographic principles, thoughts become your Reality. The Monroe Institute, founded by Robert Monroe, uses Hemi-Sync techniques involving sound waves to entrain brain waves called the Gateway Experience. Entraining is the continuous nature of an action. The Gateway Experience lets the right hemisphere bypass the left hemisphere, altering human consciousness.[xxvi]

According to the theories of Carl Pribram, a neuroscientist at Stanford, and David Baum, a physicist at the University of London, the human mind is also a hologram. The human mind attunes to the universal hologram, and a transfer of information occurs, resulting in our daily experiences. Microtubules in the brain may perform a similar function as a laser to create a holographic image. Lasers are the purest form of light available to us and send out a beam of waves in a single frequency. For example, laser waves are like the ripples made by a pebble gently dropped in a pond.

The CIA paper further elaborates that a holographic image is created in space via an interference pattern. An interference pattern results from the interactions between energy in motion (bit 1) and energy at rest (bit 0). Energy at rest is "matter" that visualizes the desired result via the hippocampus in the left hemisphere. The hippocampus regions are where the brain sends a projection we visualize holographically. Energy in motion is energy that feels the desired result in the right hemisphere.

Limbic system

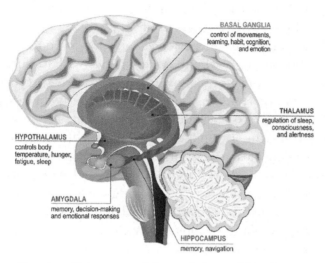

Quantum Being- a conduit to a holographic universe

When we visualize an image via our mind, we use our left hemisphere hippocampus to imagine and project. Our left hemisphere acts like a transmitter that follows the Binary Computing System where Energy in Rest = 0 indicates Potential Energy like matter representing two-Dimensional Data. The potential energy is the energy of what can be. On the other hand, our right hemisphere is non-linear and acts like a receptor that receives and feels the desired result with Emotion = Energy in Motion = 1 indicating Kinetic Energy representing three-Dimensional Data. Kinetic energy is the energy of what is.

Biofeedback teaches the left hemisphere to visualize the desired result and teaches the right hemisphere to recognize the feelings associated with the visualization. This is how the left brain is in tune with the right brain creating a state of coherence. In this way, the pathways are strengthened and emphasized so that the left-brain consciousness can access appropriate areas in the right brain using a conscious, demand mode. Neuro-linguistic programming (NLP) works due to biofeedback based on a connection between neurological processes (neuro), language (linguistic), and behavioral patterns learned through experience (programming). NLP programming is tailored to individual needs to achieve specific goals in life.

Per the Gateway Experience, an out-of-body experience makes the body's energy field homogeneous with its surrounding environment. It promotes movement of the seat of consciousness into the surrounding environment partly in response to the fact that the two electromagnetic medians are now a single energy continuum. Brain hemisphere synchronization enables human consciousness to establish a coherent pattern of perception in dimensions where speeds below Planck's distance, 10^{-33} centimeters per second, apply, creating a step out of time and space. Bentov clarifies, "Quantum mechanics tell us that when the speed of the oscillation drops below Planck's distance, we enter, in effect, a new world."

An out-of-body experience interprets holographic energy patterns given off by people or things interacting in time-space reality, enabling us to interface with dimensions beyond time and space. This is when we enter a new world.

To understand consciousness, we need to understand what happens during out-of-body experiences. For example, we have heard of people having out-of-body experiences who have accelerated and enhanced their consciousness to experience dimensions beyond the physical.

During an "out-of-body" experience, a person perceives the world from a location outside their physical body, a different vantage point. An out-of-body experience generally happens under extreme circumstances and is self-induced without prior experience. For example, an out-of-body experience can help in traumatic situations by separating your mind from the body experiencing physical trauma.

An out-of-body experience can save a life. My friend was able to initiate an out-of-body experience at will when she was kidnapped and about to experience sexual assault. Through an out-of-body experience, she was able to see and experience more than usual. The perpetrator was caught because she saw the gun license number while "sitting" in a tree a short distance away from him during her out-of-body experience.

Dr. Fenwick studied 1,500 heart patients to prove the out-of-body experience is a real phenomenon. He placed objects in the ER room that the patient couldn't see or know about. Based on his findings, the mind and brain are not the same things; they are separate. There is a lot of evidence to show that consciousness lives outside of the brain. Telepathy can be another way to prove it.[xxvii]

Ayahuasca can induce an out-of-body experience. Dr. Frank Echenhofer wanted to understand and scientifically prove how Ayahuasca, used socially and ceremonially as spiritual medicine among the indigenous peoples of the Amazon basin, affects consciousness. Ayahuasca is a South American psychoactive brew referred to as a wine of the soul. This plant-based psychedelic affects all senses and enables multi-dimensional travel based on various witnesses documented over many years. Dr. Frank put himself through the Ayahuasca experience with an EEG (Electroencephalogram) attached to see all his neuron activities. After 30 minutes of the intake, he started feeling the effect. He traveled to other places based on the graphs recorded in his EEG. Dr. Frank started moving his hand like he was choreographing an orchestra. His brain was in an enhanced state of consciousness. His graph mirrors the out-of-body EEGs recorded of other out-of-body experiences.[xxviii]

> *An out-of-body experience is a projection of an eternal spark of consciousness and memory. This eternal spark is the soul, an energy pattern depicted by the pattern of the Flower of Life and a representation of human consciousness.*

To expand on Immanuel Kant's description of space and time being the frameworks that constrain the mind to its version of Reality, we need to understand what time is.

Time is Relative

We tune in to a moment based on our thoughts. Time passes linearly from our perspective, our beliefs, and the consensus Reality we live in. Therefore, we look at the clock or calendar to keep our understanding of time being linear as a whole truth.

Time is absolutely essential to schedule events, meet another person, or perform a critical task. We don't feel time. We only experience it based on our age and what the calendar shows. Per Mike Dooley, TIME is an acronym for "Trace each other Into Material Existence," and space is used for projection only.

Time is linear, divided into the past, present, and future. The only way we can understand time is in the third physical dimension. Linear time shows the past, present, and future due to entropy, the movement from order to disorder. Low entropy allows correlation and memory to build in one direction and not the other. Entropy is simply a measure of chaos and disorder. It affects all aspects of our daily lives, on both a macro and a microscopic level. The more disordered something is, the more entropic we consider it.

The second law of thermodynamics states that the total entropy of an isolated system always increases over time. The key to understanding how our brain inherits the arrow of time lies in comprehending the connection between entropy and correlation.

> *Entropy is directly proportional to time,*
> *correlation, and chaos.*

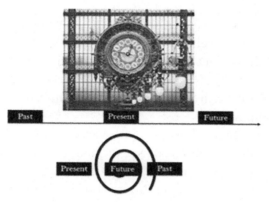

What if you take a straight line and twist it to a spiral?
What happens to Time then?
Past, Present, And Future can interject and interconnect at the same time.
Time is a perspective

What if you take the straight line and twist it into a spiral? What happens to time, then? Past, present, and future can interject and interconnect simultaneously. Time in the past doesn't exist. We only access stored memory by retrieving the internal and external memory explained in Chapter 8, "Intelligent Architecture." Intrinsic memory uses information stored in our DNA and can also be obtained by the morphogenetic field, also known as the Akashic field. Since time is continuously changing due to ongoing thoughts and actions in the present, time doesn't exist in the future. Therefore, time travel in that sense doesn't work.

> *We may be hopping timelines, but not time.*

For example, the speed of thought travels faster than the speed of light. The data is all there. We are only accessing the "read head" like in a gramophone. A read head is a part of a recording device that senses data on a carrier medium. Therefore, time travel is simply a matter of relocating the read head to point to different points along the timeline.

The most advanced part of the universal quantum process is how the brain comprehends and measures the flow of time with the past and the uncertain future in the form of electrical activity. This process is universal and interactive, from the largest object to the smallest creature, right down to the microscopic elements of the periodic table.

Time is not linear because with each moment of consciousness continuing on a different set of memories and experiences, it wouldn't matter if our timeline is completely scrambled. We wouldn't notice it due to our limitation in comprehension. This means if we walk in a different timeline, we still can't discern. When we watch time travel movies, we think of time still moving forward even when we visit the past era. Why is that? Our Reality is stuck in a linear mindset.

Walter Russell explains,

> "Time is continually being formed photon by photon by the spontaneous absorption and emission of light waves of electromagnetic radiation, a process of continuous change, and continuous energy exchange, forming the future uncertainty of everyday life."

This uncertainty can be seen mathematically through Heisenberg's uncertainty principle of quantum physics, which is mentioned earlier in the book. It states that we can't simultaneously discern both the momentum and position of a particle since matter is always in formation within the physical world.

Time is how we perceive experiences. When we say time heals all things, it truly means we heal everything, ultimately by bringing light to the situation. In the quantum world, we can instantaneously heal lifelong trauma by turning the bit 1 to bit 0 in a nanosecond. Manifestation works faster in a quantum state because time is an illusion. Traveling back in time and substituting a bad memory with a good one for healing is the key to updating our versions. When we are sick, we can simply tap into other healthy feelings and hop timelines. It is not easy, but it will help to expedite healing. Fake it till you make it sometimes works. Except I am asking you to believe in it rather than faking it.

In the 70s, physicists devised another experiment called "The Delayed Choice Quantum Eraser." This experiment measures photons' light particles after choosing to take one path or superposition of multiple paths. The experiment proved what Niels Bohr had from the Copenhagen interpretation mentioned earlier, stating that anything unobserved would be in a wave-like state of quantum superposition. The findings showed, "It makes no difference whether we delay the measurement or not; as long as we measure the photon's path before it arrives at a detector, we still lose the interference pattern." The effect seemed to precede the cause. The Delayed Choice Quantum Eraser experiment questions our understanding of linear time.

The Delayed Choice Quantum Eraser experiment concluded that consciousness impacts the outcome even before it is applied. The sheer act of noticing, rather than any physical disturbance, can cause the collapse. Therefore, making life decisions is similar to having a superposition of multiple states with various outcomes.

> *This means once we decide to do something, we launch that reality with our attention, thoughts, and consciousness. Then everything is directed to manifest a quantum collapse to make it happen. That is why intention becomes the driving force for manifestation.*

Based on Einstein's theory of relativity, time is relative.

Time is affected by:

1. The observer's perspective.
2. The speed at which an observer is moving.
3. Applied gravitational force based on the observer's position with respect to Earth.

The Observer's Perspective:

An observer in motion experiences time dilation, meaning that time moves more slowly when someone is moving than when someone is standing still. Therefore, based on relativity, a person moving ages slower than a person at rest. This is why when we are in a crucial moment in our life, everything stops and becomes a slow-motion movie. When you are doing something you love, time passes differently because your sense of time changes.

> *Time dilation is experienced when we are in the flow, one with everything around us.*

The book "Seth Speaks" states the following about time:

> *"You are presently focused not only in your physical body but within a particular frequency of events that you interpret as time. You spend all your time examining this one small stream so that you become hypnotized by its flow and entranced by its motion."*

The Observer's Speed:

When astronaut Scott Kelly flew for 340 consecutive days on the International Space Station (ISS), his twin brother, astronaut

Mark Kelly, living on Earth, aged a little faster than Scott. For 25 months, 10 research teams subjected the twins to a battery of tests, including blood, urine, and feces samples before, during, and after the spaceflight. Mark ate, drank, and did whatever he wanted. In contrast, Scott was subject to a strict diet and exercise regimen aboard the space station. *"Scott's telomeres mysteriously lengthened during spaceflight,"* says Susan Bailey, a radiation cancer biologist at Colorado State University in Fort Collins. Generally, telomeres shorten with age, and spaceflight stresses the body. Scott's telomeres did revert back in 48 hours to pre-flight lengths, making him one year younger than his brother Mark.[xxix]

Space and time tilt into each other, so different observers slice up blocks of time at different angles depending on their velocities. Even your sense of the present changes with your motion. Start moving now, and your "slice of now" is skewed. The future becomes your present, and the things you left behind milliseconds ago have passed. Imagine that the future is created as a wave of the present sweeping out the block universe.

> **This means your present is setting the stage for your future to emerge.**

Gravity:

The only thing that can move across dimensions like time is gravity. Time is an effect we perceive as gravity, and the stronger gravity is, the slower time passes. So, gravity is inversely proportional to time. Scientists experimented to understand the relationship between Earth's gravitational force and time using an atomic clock. They realized time moved faster when it was away from Earth's gravitational force.

Sir Roger Penrose believed that gravity converts quantum behavior to normal behavior via microtubules, a molecular structure in our brains. We can infer that the microtubule in the brain performs a similar function as a laser by creating a holographic image.

To continue our quest of expanding consciousness, we need to understand what drives consciousness.

Microtubule Causing Collapse

Sir Roger Penrose, also working beside Dr. Stuart Hammeroff, has discovered molecular structures within microtubules that can alter their state in response to a single quantum event. Their research statement explains,

> *"Quantum superposition has something to do with how neurons are triggered to communicate via electrical signals. Each neuron is filled with small structures called microtubules inside the cell. These microtubules are lattice polymers inside the cell and pretty much run the show from mitosis to synaptic information to plasticity to storing the info. Their role is to increase the capacity of the brain."*

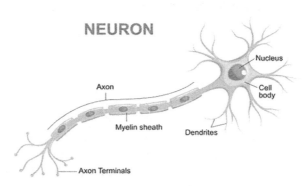

Microtubules inside the brain

Microtubules are molecular assemblies. They're cylindrical polymers composed of repeating patterns of a single, peanut-shaped protein called tubulin that can flex "open" and "closed" every nanosecond. This tubulin acts as a microscopic computer driven by quantum processes. The tubulin proteins self-assemble into these beautifully elegant hollow cylinders with walls arranged in hexagonal lattices following a Fibonacci geometry.[xxx, xxxi]

Our nervous system sends signals via electricity. The flow of electrons is the smallest unit of matter in the universe. This is what creates electricity. The microtubules communicate with each other similar to how a computer would communicate with other computers on the same network. Isn't it amazing how intricate our internal computing system is? Far more complex than the computers we have designed so far!

Sir Roger Penrose and Dr. Stuart have proven that *"Microtubules in the human brain have evolved into a specific configuration that allows a natural process occurring in space-time geometry at the Planck-scale level to happen in a way that also involves cognition, computation, and intelligence."* Their theory and experiments also prove that microtubules create consciousness by facilitating approximately 40 "quantum wave function collapses" per second. This means we have 40 possibilities of realities within a second. We can direct the collapse with our thoughts, intentions, and whatever memory we access. We genuinely have a lot more choices than we give ourselves credit for.

Wolf Singer's gamma synchrony is evidence of quantum-state collapses happening 40 times per second—or more—among coherent, organized networks of the brain's microtubules. Coherence is related to "frequency and amplitude." Singer discovered Gamma synchrony in 1980s Germany while experimenting with highly sensitive EEG machines. Typically, with an EEG, you get squiggly lines on the display showing your delta, theta, alpha, and beta waves ranging from zero to about 30 hertz, or waves per second. To add to his surprise, Singer discovered a higher, perfectly coherent frequency for gamma synchrony, which ranged from 30 to 90 hertz, and sometimes even higher. Forty hertz is generally typical.

This perfect electrical synchrony is the best marker we have for a neural correlation of consciousness in the brain. For example, when there's a car accident and the car is spinning, people often report that time seems to slow down. The outside world appears to move half as fast as it usually does. This could be because their rate of gamma synchrony is changing from around 40 hertz to 80 hertz. And similarly, someone once asked Michael Jordan, when he was in his prime, how he could outperform the other team so well. He said when he's playing, *"well, it's like the other team is in slow motion."* So, maybe Michael Jordan was experiencing 60, 70, or 80 conscious moments per second, and the defense was only experiencing something like 40.

Escaping Illusion

The idea of enlightenment means to escape the illusion. Quantum mechanics demonstrates that time experienced results from quantum collapse within infinite probabilities and possibilities.

> *Any perception of time and continuity is an illusion.*

Time in the present is an illusion. Present time is never observable due to how fast light travels and how slow our mind processes information. In short, the present we experience is an illusion due to the amount of time light takes to reflect off of matter and how our mind processes information. However, the experience we feel is Real.

Have you ever fallen in love? Have you been distracted by the projection of what you want to see in the person versus who they truly are? Why is that? Because our imagination of the person's potential has a stronger resonance than physical Reality. Messages are carried via resonance, the foundation of quantum physics. Actions do speak louder than words. However, when we are blinded by love, we deny physical Reality. We keep reinforcing our imagination on what is happening right in front of us, hoping they will match one day. We are often disappointed because we are distracted by an illusion.

When we break the illusion, we realize the truth that "life is messy." What we see on social media, Facebook, Instagram, etc., being portrayed as a perfect life is not, in Reality, perfect. Is it? If we walked into someone's life and shadowed them by being invisible, we would see their Real life. True life! And then, as we peek into their emotions, feelings, hurt, pain, and innate joy, we would better understand the person. *"The illusion of the self must remain an illusion until the self is surrendered"* is a quote from the book *"The Human Aura."*

Sir Roger Penrose and Dr. Stuart have proven that consciousness is illusory since activity related to consciousness appears to occur too late. Consciousness perception involves three waves from the thalamus due to the correlation with anesthesia. Consciousness occurs between 300 and 500 milliseconds. However, we respond consciously too early, within 30 to 100 milliseconds. We can't account for consciousness and free will occurring after 100 milliseconds have passed, between 300 and 500 milliseconds.[xxxii]

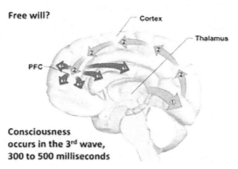

Consciousness response time

This Bashar, channeled by Darryl Anka, quote expands on our illusory world very well:

> *"All things exist at once, separated by frequencies experienced as a timeframe. The continuity we*

*experience is an illusion created to experience space-
time Reality. We are choosing the timeframe related
to one another based on the relevance to the theme
we choose to explore on Earth."*

Basically, Bashar is saying that we perceive time while, in truth, we are experiencing a Reality of our choosing based on the frequencies we vibrate at every moment.

According to *The Matrix* movie, it means taking the red pill. The more we realize how illusory the world is around us, the better off we are in making the right choices. This is similar to being in the Matrix, where Reality is different than our perception; however, pain, joy, and all our experiences are real. Therefore, we should take the world around us seriously, not literally.

Speaking of illusion, Elon Musk is vocal about us living in a simulation. Let's imagine for a minute that our Reality is a virtual game, and we are the users and architects of this game. All the parameters of the game are input by our thoughts, beliefs, and subconscious programming. Every morning we wake up and start playing our live video game.

Dr. Donald Hoffman, a Department of Cognitive Sciences professor who studies consciousness and visual perception, suggests that we are interfacing with a graphical user interface (GUI), a virtual headset attached to our forehead, in an awakened state. Generally, a GUI is a visual way of interacting with a computer using windows, icons, and menus within the operating systems.[xxxiii]

We are creating circumstances through our GUIs to help us process all our reflections explained in the "Mirror, Mirror" chapter. *Contact* depicts a classic example of how GUI works in our daily life. In the movie *Contact*, mentioned in Chapter 10, Jodie Foster travels to the planet that an alien has sent a radio signal from, and she passes through a wormhole. She then finds herself on a beach, similar to a childhood picture she drew of Pensacola, Florida. The first figure to approach her was her deceased father. Jodie Foster's character, Dr. Ellie, recognizes her father as an alien. The alien had taken on her father's form and was asking questions. The alien tells her that the familiar landscape and form are used to make their first contact easier. This is an example of how we can architect our GUI for our evolution.

The power of the mind is how Wim Hof operates. He has become an iconic mentor and teacher, inspiring people to do things they would ordinarily find very uncomfortable or consider impossible. My oldest son follows this method, so when we visited Paris in 2017, I had people stop me, concerned that he was wearing only a T-shirt and shorts in November during a 30°F and freezing rain. My son was using Wim Hof's techniques to tolerate colder temperatures.

In the movie *Discovery*, a scientist uncovers that the afterlife exists. He can monitor and record another plane of existence through brain waves at a subatomic level. There was a peculiarity in his findings because dead people traveled to an alternate reality with similar lives; however, their role-playing was changed. They were rewriting their life scripts with positive outcomes. When you exit your old pattern and rewrite it with a new pattern, you usually end up with a new script or plane of existence. That could literally mean death and rebirth.

Consciousness directs the light cone in the form of awareness to see through the GUI. Once we can see the direct link between our thoughts and how it affects our day-to-day experiences in a quantum world, we can control our daily experiences to keep enhancing our consciousness. Conscious evolution requires us to be self-aware and show up every day in our best form to spread love.

The Great Pyramid exemplifies a level of human consciousness and is a monument to decoding human existence. If we live in a simulated world, then the Earth is the spacecraft, and the Great Pyramid holds the key to the ignition and power. The words "pyra mid" in Italian means "the fire in the middle." The Great Pyramid is an ancient structure in the form of a machine. These ancient machines were built at a particular time, in a specific space or location, in a distinct shape, and with a particular frequency for a unique purpose. This is similar to us, quantum beings on planet Earth, vibrating our frequency and light based on our unique purpose and destiny.

Astronaut Edgar Dean Mitchell, the sixth person to walk on the Moon, explains a quantum hologram as:

> "The fractals of the electromagnetic field energy interconnect with everything through multiple layers of morphogenetic fields repeating their fractal patterns in many dimensions within the universe and are the basic building blocks of the holographic universe we live in."

> *If we live in a holographic universe that follows principles of fractality to create our Reality frame by frame, we can certainly change our inputs to drive a different experience and affect our Reality.*

Understand that there is more to life than meets the eye because we are quantum in nature. Our perception plays a role in creating our day-to-day Reality, and consciousness precedes perception. When we access consciousness beyond space and time, we are open to experiencing both past and future events like time travelers. A quote from the movie "Interstellar" captures this concept: *"Love is the one thing we're capable of perceiving that transcends dimensions of time and space."*

Gamma synchrony is a gauge for being in the zone, being in the flow, and experiencing oneness all around us like "bliss." This bliss is a powerful state for healing since our DNA gets discretely reprogrammed and aligned to experience bliss. It is a game-changer when it comes to transformation.

The "Life and Teaching of the Masters of the Far East" explained, *"Man will realize as Jacob did that the real gate to Heaven is through his consciousness."* As we continually expand our understanding of ourselves and consciously evolve, we rewrite our life script.

Choosing our most fulfilling dream to unfold the next level of evolution is the key to living a purposeful life. It is the key to dialing into the desired dimension and frequency in every moment of life. Achieving the highest level of excitement is the frequency that allows us to explore and evolve.

Consciousness is the ability to be present in your life in every moment, without judgment from yourself or anyone else. It is the ability to receive everything, reject nothing, and create everything you desire in life — greater than what you currently have and more than what you can imagine.

Imagine with GUI

1. Create a visual image of what my GUI looks like that I create daily.
2. What input can I change to the GUI to ensure a different or better outcome?
3. How is my GUI showing up daily? (Tweak my inputs as needed.)
4. What patterns perpetuate this "imagination" to keep it in a physical form?
5. What patterns don't serve me any longer? Should I release them?

Reprogramming Subconscious Guidelines:

We operate from 95% subconscious (autonomous behavior) and 5% conscious (learned behavior).

> ### *Let's all be Life Programmers!*

1. Stop old talk and old programming.
2. Put in a new program. This is our opportunity to rewrite anything we want.
3. Repeat. Repetition will help reprogram our subconscious minds.

Barometer Test

We are a consciousness barometer. Visit a crowded place and see whom you attract based on your vibration and frequency. See what you have in common and what you don't.

Test it out when you are at the airport. Try only interacting with people with whom you feel an easy exchange of energy. The rest of the people are invisible to you, and you are invisible to them. This is because your vibration and frequency are not matching theirs right now.

Scan the code above with you smart phone to view
a message from Shehnaz – or follow this link:

https://youtu.be/V_KowsPAJsI

Chapter 12

Magickal Spark

*When we avail the Magickal spark within us,
we unveil the secrets of manifestation.*
—Shehnaz Soni

*I*magination gives birth to life. The word Magick is embedded in imagination. Do we need different filters in the lenses of our telescopes to see the entire Magickal universe? What if we could see the world in its entirety? What if there were no limitations to our sight and our hearing? What if we could wear the glasses from the *Spiderwick* movie and see invisible things? If that were to happen, we would not need any computer game for distraction because the waking world would be very Magickal, just as it is. In fact, the world is already more amazing than meets the eyes, and our capacities are unbound as we continually expand our consciousness.

> *Magick is availing the spark to manifest
> and transform our dreams into Reality.*

What drives my will? What is that "spark" within me that makes me get out of bed and encourages me to live every day? What excites me? Our human "will" can tap into the undiscovered realm and manifest our dreams. This is why we say, *"When there is a will, there is a way."* This is where all the Magick happens.

> *Spark is a trace of an intense feeling in our soul that shines through our eyes!*

Spark is the "will" in our consciousness. With Mystery School teachings, there is a powerful mantra. *"It's by will alone, I set my mind in motion."* This mantra reminds us that our w*ill* is the key that opens the door via our mind to our soul to access other dimensions, universes, and realities.

Magick

Magick is "alchemy," the ancient study and philosophy of changing basic substances such as metals into other substances. Alchemy is in action in the kitchen, where we use tools like a knife to transform the food.

The philosophers' stone was the central symbol of the mystical terminology of alchemy, symbolizing perfection at its finest. It was highly valued due to the properties it carried as the elixir of life, beneficial for rejuvenation and for achieving immortality. How mythical it is, depends on your beliefs.

According to the "science of transformation," there are two alchemical processes:

1. Physical alchemy is altering and transforming the properties within matter.
2. Spiritual alchemy is freeing your spiritual self-trapped within you due to the unrefined parts of yourself that house fears, personal beliefs, and self-doubt.

When we go through a physical transformation due to disease, surgery, or fitness, we shed the extra weight we carry in the form of matter. We transform ourselves both physically and mentally. This is why we must be gentle and kind with ourselves while we are simultaneously healing all our layers. We are chiseling away what doesn't serve us and making a "sigil" out of our human crafts as quantum beings.

Sigil holds our manifestation

A sigil is an intention-charged symbol of a desired goal and serves as a Magickal tool. You can make your own sigil and program it to represent a goal.

Magick is a powerful energy that can be stored, magnified, and even brought to a critical mass for use as a bomb. The documentary "Absolute Magick" suggests that Magick can be explained with logic and science if well understood. What is the difference between Magick and science? Science manipulates physical matter, while Magick manipulates energy. If you have the opportunity, watch this YouTube video to see the manipulation.

Iron Filings

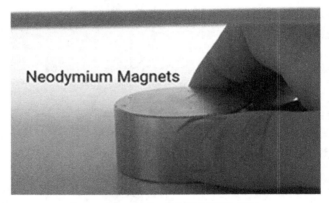

Neodymium Magnets

https://youtu.be/LMFAOLKaYd0

Is there a difference between Magick and science?

When we sprinkle the iron filing on top of the glass and use the neodymium magnets to control the shape and direction of the iron filings, they move as we intended. It can be construed as Magick and yet is still explained by science. Magick precedes science. What is Magick today will be explained by science tomorrow.

Magick operates on three principles:

1. The willpower of the individual: intention/the why behind the thought or idea.
2. The actual material basis: matter, quantum being, and words since words carry energy.

3. The actual force upon which the mind operates to effect the change in material.

1-Will Power – Intention:

When we combine "will" with "force," we call it "willpower." As an alchemist, we set foot in the laboratory, and we decide what we want to create. The critical driver behind any creation is intention. The intention is essential to deliver a spark. The intention births the idea that you intend to carry out. The intention is the underlying cause behind your goal, purpose, or aim.

The intention should never be judged by you. For example, if you are going to the gym to be healthy and fit and spend more quality time with your kids, that's an intention. If you are going to the gym to look appealing and have a better option for attracting a mate, that's another intention. No intention is better than the other. The key here is that your resulting manifestation is interwoven with your intention. Therefore, being true to yourself about your intention is essential for the ultimate outcome of your manifestation.

We are all human, so our unique conditioning will always affect our outcomes. That's why we are a work-in-progress. Regardless, our intention is embedded in everything we do, whether we are conscious of it or not. Therefore, actively making intentions expedites the overall outcome of our manifestation.

Here are a few points to consider to implement your intentions in your daily life. When you start a new project, direction, hobby, etc., tune into your inner navigational system. Engage in self-talk to understand yourself, then clearly state your intention without judgment. Bashar says, *"All is here now. Manifestation allows us to tune into a certain frequency moment-to-moment based on our compass needle that points to our magnetic north."* The intention is the key to manifestation. Therefore, having an honest and clear intention will drive a rewarding experience in the form of manifestation.

Intention is used in space exploration as well. Voyager 1 and 2, built by the Jet Propulsion Laboratory- JPL, were launched by

NASA about 42 years ago. The Voyager's primary intent was to conduct close-up studies of Jupiter, Saturn, Saturn's rings, and the large moons of the two planets. To accomplish their two-planet mission, JPL built the spacecraft to last five years. Voyager 1 lasted longer than any other spacecraft in history. It provided scientists with never-before-seen observations of our boundary with interstellar space. About 35 years later, it continues to collect data that exceeds expectations compared to the initial intent. Sharing the Voyager story above clarifies how manifestation can be magnificent and beyond our imagination. Therefore, be open to receiving miracles.[xxxiv]

The power of intention is also used in healing in an experiment called *The Wounded Leaf*. The experiment was performed to change the glow of a leaf by combining a remote viewing principle and an intention principle. It was documented in Lynn McTaggart's *The Field*. The leaf was viewed by a group of people who combined visualizing and intending principles to heal the leaf. In this case, the injured leaf grew brighter due to biophoton emission, and all the punctured holes were filled with light. We, as quantum beings, can affect the glow of the leaf.[xxxv]

Just imagine how we can affect our human craft when we direct healing energies with loving intention. If our intention can heal the leaf that was not even in close proximity, imagine what we can do to our own body with intention. If we genuinely want to heal ourselves, we *can* improve our health. We are more powerful than we give ourselves credit for.

2-Material:

The human body is full of crystals. The crystal is a known quantum amplifier since it can transmit energy in a magnified form. The crystal in our bodies is microtubule in structure. Microtubules are photon conductors, and photon conductors emit and absorb light and twist in a spiral pattern. Per Chief Golden Light Eagle, who was a leader in the field of star knowledge channeled to him via star beings, we have 18 crystals on each side of the body. We have crystals in our brain, lungs, kidneys, and reproductive system.

We have magnetite clusters around the pineal gland within our brain. Magnetite is a crystal linking our intuitive state to the natural world around us. The electromagnetic connection to our mind via the magnetite and pineal system navigates information received by electromagnetic waves to connect us with all there is.[xxxvi]

We also have microscopic crystals residing in our inner ears. These crystals are called otoconia. Otoconia are bio-crystals essential for us to sense linear acceleration and gravity to maintain physical balance.

Even our teeth are growing crystals, with the enamel around it being the hardest substance on Earth.

Our skull and bones are made of a crystal called calcium carbonate.

When we make love, we feel intense feelings because we create a piezoelectricity phenomenon inside our bodies, just like orgonite. Orgonite is used to cleanse negative energy and counteract the effects electromagnetic waves have on our bodies. Therefore, making love can truly enhance our health and manifestation with intention. Per Paulo Coelho, *"When you have an intense contact of love with nature or another human being, like a spark, then you understand that there is no time and that everything is eternal."*

3-Force:

When we apply stimuli to crystals, it forces them to offer up their embedded information energy, to which all things are connected, including the wave particles within the crystals. This is how the holographic universe comes into form. This force is an agent of life or light by which animated beings are rendered magnetic. The practice of Kabbalah is attributed to this latent electricity within us. Tesla confirms, *"We are electricity in human form."* Therefore, photons that exist inside our very own DNA may be the driving force behind the alteration of our genetic structure.

Having multiple near-death experiences of my own has made me highly aware of the power inside me, which has kept me alive. One occurred when I was 11 years old. I was visiting Hawkes Bay Beach in Karachi per our weekly ritual. As a girl growing up in Pakistan, I never learned any sports or swimming. I was only allowed to get my feet wet. I was singing and playing in the water and in my own world. Suddenly, a wave came and swept me away. It kept sweeping me away farther and farther, and I had no control over my petite body. I started witnessing my life flash right in front of my eyes like a movie. The movie flash displayed all the events that were significant to me from the present until I was in my mother's womb. I passed out. I didn't remember anything else. My father, being a great swimmer, saved me from drowning and gave me CPR to bring me back to life. I was supposed to live to be here now to share all I have learned and accomplished. Our time on Earth is limited but purposeful.

What makes people live through extreme conditions like being abandoned at sea for months or stranded in a blizzard in the middle of nowhere? What keeps them going when the odds are against them, and they run into situations that bring them very close to death, yet they still survive? There is a force within us that is beyond our comprehension yet very powerful.

Magician Eliphas Levi reinforces the same message,

> *"The force is fluid in nature and would receive the vibrations of the will via meditation. It is a force acted upon by the frequency of thought. This force illuminates the mind, vivifies, destroys, separates, and coagulates all depending on the will of the individual."*

Thought that leads to imagination and planning that leads to action.

Jesus reinforced this in the book "Life and Teaching of the Masters of the Far East." *"I have one mode of expression, and that is through an **idea, thought, word, and action**."* One mode of expression is divided into four steps. The Kabbalistic Tree of Life has four worlds aligning with a similar strategy for manifestation.

1. Idea: The first spark, goal, destiny, a light bulb moment.
2. Thought: Visualization and imagination fill in the detail with emotion and feelings of love.
3. Plan: Words spoken or written. Understand the critical steps in achieving the right words to reprogram your subconscious.
4. Action: Experience your manifestation.

Where does this force – inner drive reside? Within our soul? Crystals are just as unique in their energetic signatures that are formed in many configurations and facets reflected through a human being's individualized soul experience.

Soul

Per Kabbalistic teaching, a human's different aspects of existence are connected via soul to a silver cord. This silver cord is connected to the limitless light coming through the crown chakra where spirit, our higher self, resides. Our bodies, minds, and emotions encompassed within human craft are the vessels for the light of the soul. The quote that perfectly connects to the spiritual journey via the Kabbalistic principle is, *"The spirit clothes itself to come down and unclothes itself to go up."*

Kabbalistic teaching refers to Ashim, Order of the Angels, meaning the soul of fire, considered the atomic consciousness holding physical matter together. Ashim, the spark, represents the natural consciousness of dense matter.

The book "Seth Speaks" states the following about the soul:

> *"The soul is alive, responsive, curious. It forms the flesh and the world you know, and it gives in a state of becoming. The soul is the most highly motivated, most highly energized, and most potent conscious- ness unit known in any universe. Atoms speak and call themselves by name. Our physical body is a field of energy with a certain form."*

The soul weighs about 21 grams (less than an ounce) accord- ing to Dr. Duncan McDougall, a Boston physician, in 1907. He used a delicate and precise measurement scale on six people who died in order to perform an experiment. He discovered an average 21 grams change in body weight upon death. Since our soul is the spark that keeps us alive and leaves us when we die, it is similar to a genie escaping the bottle.

Regardless of the accuracy of the weight of the soul, the bot- tom-line message is that our soul leaves our body when we die. A soul has a mass that gets transformed into light or spirit energy and is reunited with the unified field all around us. We can refer to it as a morphogenetic field.[xxxvii]

Contrary to ancient, sacred teachings, scientists believed that the soul is in the brain. However, it has been challenging to prove this, given the complexity of the billions of neurons in the brain. According to the 17th-century philosopher Rene Descartes, *"I think therefore I am"* is an acknowledgment of our self-awareness and the existence of the soul. This self-cognition is what distin- guishes us from the plant and animal kingdoms. Rene Descartes believed that the pineal gland is the seat of the soul, the place where the realms of thoughts and feelings intersect with the physical brain. Maybe that is why autopsies on spiritual people have revealed a larger pineal gland. Perhaps the third eye assists them in accessing a higher vision.

Neuroscience believes the mind and the brain are connected. Dr. Adrian Owen wanted to understand the boundary of consciousness. He performed an experiment on a woman in a vegetative state to test her consciousness. Dr. Owen asked her to imagine moving from room to room to exercise and test her spatial navigation. This command is known to activate an area deep inside the healthy brain cell called the parahippocampal gyrus, based on Dr. Owen's 20-year research. The woman's brain responded the same as a healthy brain. Dr. Owen proved that despite no signs of outward awareness, for some humans, an inner spark remains undiscovered within the brain.[xxxviii]

Contrary to Dr. Owen's discovery, ancient Egyptians and many other ancient tribes believed that the soul resided in the heart, which is why it is treated with more respect than the brain. However, it is very interesting to consider people with heart transplants. It has been reported that they take on the personality and memory of the heart donor, including having similar dreams to ones the donor used to have. We also know that the heart is 100 times stronger electrically and thousands of times stronger magnetically compared to the brain.

Knowing where the soul resides can be enhanced by understanding how anesthesia works. Anesthesia selectively erases consciousness while sparing other brain functions. According to Dr. Stuart,

> *"There is no dream or consciousness under anesthesia since the passage of time is the key feature of consciousness, and under anesthesia, the patient doesn't register elapsed time. During anesthesia, a brain scanner reveals that when a bright, flashing halogen light is used, this helps stimulate the brain response. This bright light pierces through the taped eyelid. EEGs show the patient is responding just as if they were awake."*

I have been under anesthesia various times, and I have loved the sensation when surgery is over. The sensation of not having to endure the pain and still fix my human craft.[xxxix]

The human body dies after five minutes with no oxygen. What happens during that time? Dr. Peter Fenwick, a neuropsychiatrist, states that consciousness can separate from the brain by retaining information in near-death cardiac arrest and returning to the person if they die. This means that consciousness may reside in the body in a way that is not entirely dependent on the brain for its functioning. This has been proven in studies of people who are in comas.[xl]

This theory aligns with Dr. Stuart's understanding of consciousness being entangled with the quantum world and accessible outside the body. Dr. Stuart's fascination with understanding consciousness enabled him to have a "eureka" moment when he found that microtubules are the location of the soul. His words were, *"Microtubules are the origin of consciousness. Specifically, quantum computation synchronized to gamma EEG inside the neurons in the brain is the origin of consciousness."* It is conceivable for Dr. Stuart that when a patient has a cardiac arrest or dies, the quantum information that involves consciousness is not destroyed. On the contrary, consciousness is actually leaked out to the universe and remains entangled and can revert back if the patient is brought back to life. It continues to exist at the Planck scale, yet remains entangled as a certain pattern, at least temporarily. So, if the patient is revived, the quantum pattern gets drawn back into the microtubules inside the brain, and the patient reports having had a near-death or out-of-body experience. If the patient dies, then it is conceivable that the quantum information can remain entangled in some sort of afterlife state. And perhaps the data can get pulled back into a new creature, a zygote or embryo, in which case you'd have something like reincarnation. Therefore, the soul is an actual physical entity in terms of quantum information embedded in the fundamental level of the universe.[xli]

Babylon 5, a great science fiction series, has a scene where Ambassador Delenn is asked a question about what she believes. She responds, *"Soul is a non-localized phenomenon."* A non-localized vector is a vector that requires only its magnitude and direction for its description. According to Delenn, *"The soul is projected through our body; our body is not a soul. For example, if we project a beam of light on a wall, the wall is just a medium to perceive light. The wall is not a source of light. Similarly, the soul is just a projection through our body. The universe is conscious and beyond our perception. We are the universe trying to understand itself."* What if our soul is projected via hologram in the form of us and everything around us? This would let us choose what we look like in the afterlife.[xlii]

Based on my lifelong learning, the soul resides within our physical body, and the spirit resides within our non-physical body.

- Our soul is a bridge and transformer between spirit and body.
- Our spirit is our non-physical essence that resides within the outer layer of our aura.

Do you wonder what happens to all the learning we have accomplished in our human body? Does it all go to waste? The answer is "No." Based on ancient sacred teachings, there are three permanent seed atoms located in:

1. Pineal Gland around the third eye, for mental teaching
2. Thymus gland in the heart, for physical teaching
3. Adrenal Gland in the Solar Plexus, for emotional teaching

These permanent seed atoms contain all the DNA information for the soul to be transferred back and forth as we transform into human being form. The Lisa Renee's ascension glossary states,

> *"The permanent seed atom is that which contains the divine Christos blueprint and its blood record within the thymus gland in the higher heart center. The divine blueprint transmits the DNA fire letters into the instructional grids once relayed through the opened and activated permanent seed atom. As every living thing has a permanent seed atom and*

*blueprint structure, so do the living universal layers
of the time matrix. As the record of the permanent
seed atom opens into each sub-band and its harmonic layers across all space, time, and dimension,
it then feeds the source energy, the zero-point field,
into each of these grid's instruction layers."*

People who believe in reincarnation also believe in the existence of the soul. This is because thousands of cases have been
reported where the memory of past lives led people to places not
possible without any prior physical connection in this life. Video
games imitate our lives; therefore, people become easily addicted
to them. For example, games like "Call of Duty" depict the reincarnation aspect of life.

Why is it so essential to understand the soul and where it
resides? Because the soul is the reason we are called quantum
beings. This critical factor discerns us from artificial intelligence
(AI).

AI versus Quantum Beings

If the soul resides in the brain, then as a software engineer, I
can see that we can write algorithms to replicate the soul. These
algorithms can work via machine-learning neural networks and
deep learning to model all the neurons almost exactly in an
artificial brain to create an artificial intelligence very similar to
humans.

If that were to happen, AIs and humans would become hard
to discern if they were walking side by side.

Can a computer simulate all of the consciousness? Physical
laws are computationally based. The answer takes us deeper.
Math is the universal language; however, there is an aspect of
consciousness we can't comprehend that is at play. Sir Roger
Penrose states, *"There are things in mathematics that are beyond cal-
culation."* For example, quantum mechanics consists of two pieces
that are inconsistent with each other.

The Erwin Schrödinger famous equation shows how the system evolves in 10 minutes based on the initial condition. This method is computationally based.

$$\hat{H}\,\Psi = E\,\Psi$$

Hamiltonian   Energy
Operator   eigenvalue
(Energy operator)

The quantum measurement process is probabilistic instead of deterministic, and therefore, you can't compute it like the deterministic Schrödinger equation.

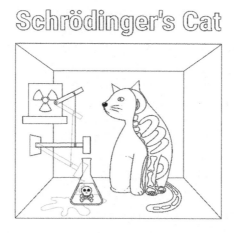

Schrödinger's Cat

Based on the Schrödinger equation, a cat can be alive or dead if placed in a closed container with an object that can kill the cat upon opening. Once we open the sealed container, we will know the state of the cat as 1 or 0. Until then, both possibilities are probabilities of existence in the quantum world. However, the cat being alive and dead at the same time directs us to a critical missing piece.[xliii]

There is a self-organizing principle at play within the measurement paradox for two inconsistencies to exist at the same time. This missing piece is why AI and a quantum being can't be the same. Sherlock Holmes says, *"When you have eliminated all which is impossible, then whatever remains, however improbable, must be the truth."*

A quantum being has the capability of applying meaning to data through intuitive and critical thinking, taking us beyond the computer algorithms used in AI. What differentiates us from artificial intelligence (AI) is the soul. Our capacity for lucid dreams also distinguishes us from AIs.

When we bring all these understandings together, we can realize how incredible the quantum being is. Our unique self-sustaining intelligence allows us to heal naturally with light over time due to our crystalline nature. We have unique capabilities to be self-aware even when we are lucid dreaming. We have the crystals inside our bodies that perform unique functions to self-heal with intention. We have the power within us to help us move a mountain if we intend to by following the three principles of Magick.

We have the soul that taps into our consciousness and can access Akashic records within the dark matter of the cosmos and help us make the right choice for future experiences. We have the alchemical process in place to make us luminous crystalline beings. This alchemy turns human lead into a luminescence crystalline matrix, the gold of the soul. We are a luminous crystalline matrix (LCM).

Khalil Gibran says, *"You have to take one step in the right direction, and your soul will unfurl itself like a lotus of countless petals."* The universe will reward you beyond your imagination. Take the first step! There is a certain momentum in that first step. The amount of motion required depends on what we want to create, but it always requires some movement! Nature, at its most fundamental level, is simply the flipping of binary digits or bits, just like a computer. We live in a binary world, so start flipping bits and see what happens!

> *Your imagination will initiate the step-by-step process toward your manifestation.*

> *We don't need to look for technology outside ourselves.*

We are the most magnificent technology! We are the conglomerations of all the technology we have experienced in our lives. We are quantum beings. We have the power to ignite our life with Magick in all aspects of our life. Recognizing our humanness and what a remarkable craft we are as quantum beings is essential for our next phase of evolution as humans on planet Earth. This recognition and realization are the first steps in living a Magickal life. So go live and let others live!

Magick of Quantum Physics

1. What is your true heart's desire providing you have:

    *   All the money you need and want.
    *   No responsibility, obligation, and expectation.
    *   No fear, guilts, regrets, past triggers.

2. What keeps you awake at night?

3. What is your intention? Why is this so important to you? Can you survive without it?

4. What is the one step you can take today that aligns you with your heart's desire and helps you change your tomorrow?

Daily Magick Rituals

➤ You can lay a quartz crystal under your pillow to have enhanced dream experiences.

➤ You can travel to places like Egypt and Peru, where your presence will become a gift you give to yourself due to the human transfiguration and DNA upgrade.

➤ You can surround yourself with people, places, and experiences that help enhance your aura due to the Vesica Pisces you make with your union.

Scan the code above with you smart phone to view a message from Shehnaz – or follow this link:

https://youtu.be/YFJBFvIj2LE

Conclusion

*"I have come a long way in my journey of self-reflection
and wisdom and am ready to receive love or
death, whichever comes first."*
—Shehnaz Soni

We all would love a fairy-tale life with a happy ending. However, life is full of spirals and obstacles. Perception, reality, and consciousness are intertwined. By understanding ourselves, we can enrich our daily manifestation and may succeed in making it a fairy tale of our choosing by transcending our dreams into Reality.

In January 2019, my life was almost taken from me. I was vulnerable, alone, and weak while quarantined in the hospital due to a misdiagnosis. I was so miserable that death seemed sweeter than living. I had a shingle in my inner eardrum. The entire team of specialists couldn't figure out the diagnosis until after I lost hearing and balance.

In this situation, I tried to take one moment at a time, hoping to see another breath. Bashar says it very well, "Every single moment, we are literally a new person." When we are tested physically due to illness or a severe health challenge, it becomes difficult to feel good and be hopeful. However, knowing we are a new person moment-to-moment can be a good reminder since our next moment doesn't have to be based on our passing moment.

This Earth is a layover place. Where we go next depends on our current evolutionary state and how well we have learned the rules of navigating life with integrity and honesty. James E. Faust says, *"Honesty is more than not lying. It is truth-telling, truth speaking, truth living, and truth loving."* Honesty is the best policy. Here is why:

1. Honesty requires less energy and more harmony.
2. Honesty helps communicate clearly and without any confusion.
3. Honesty builds trust with others.
4. Honesty with others implies honesty with yourself.

We can be proactive in creating a gratifying life by merely noticing all our goodness and appreciating it via gratitude. I live by the following quote from Gandhi, *"Happiness is when what you think, what you say, and what you do are in harmony."*

This attitude of gratitude keeps the heart open and connected to the source. Enjoy all your blessings today, and focus on everything that has refined you, helped you and upgraded you to be where you are. The universe works in a feedback loop system, and your input to the universe creates an output for your experiences, gratifications, and manifestations. Therefore "An Attitude of Gratitude" goes a long way. When you appreciate what you have, more comes back to you since it is all running in an infinite feedback loop system.

Every single atom in our body is intelligent. Our biography becomes our biology! Our thoughts affect our biology and biography via cell programming, cell communication, and cell processing. This shows up as a dance of vibration and frequency in the world of fields. The more knowledge we seek, the more we acquire, and the more self-empowered and enlightened we become.

THE QUANTUM BEING

John Steinbeck's quote sums it all up,

> *"Man is related, related inextricably to all Reality,*
> *known and unknowable. Plant a shimmering phos-*
> *phorescence on the sea and the spinning planets and*
> *an expanding universe bound together by the elastic*
> *string of time. It is advisable to look at the tide pool*
> *and the stars and look at the tide pool again."*

Nature, using the natural law of mathematics, puts itself together when left alone and creates a balance. Quantum beings similarly, can self-sustain just like crystals. When the crystal is divided, and the pieces placed side by side, the two form back together again in perfection. Understanding the quantum nature of the universe can make us realize how powerful we are as a species; therefore, we are to thrive and not just survive.

How do we create heaven on Earth? Let us define what heaven is first. Heaven is an expression of stillness that is coherent with all aspects of our existence. This multi-layered stillness is an expression of intricate music that goes on to infinity. It is a lively dance roses play to coexist with thorns.

1. What are we willing to let go of?
2. What are we not ready to let go of?
3. Our fears are the gauge to see all our attachments.
4. What price do we want to pay to coexist?
5. How can we coexist with all the duality we have around us without compromising our souls?

While taking my usual walk to a lake where alligators live, I saw a boy who looked sad. I asked him what had happened. He said an alligator ate his German Shepherd. It made me feel ill to my stomach. How can we coexist with alligators? This is where the answer lies in creating Heaven on Earth. How many trees do we want to chop down to expand our businesses? How best do we exist with all there is without creating friction and a negative ripple effect?

As a "Quantum Being," you get to decide what music you want to tune into and what frequency you want to vibrate at to make your intricate web to mark your territory. This is your Reality and how you choose to face uncomfortable moments during life's challenges. John Steinbeck states, *"It would be good to live in a perpetual state of leave-taking, never to go nor to stay, but to remain suspended in that golden emotion of love and longing; to be loved without satiety."* This is the key to quantum beingness and tapping into the infinite stillness to create coherence with all parts of ourselves to feel bliss and spiritual orgasm with all there is.

As a Quantum Being, remember to tap into the infinite zero-point energy and Akashic record daily to ride the wave of changes of your choosing while keeping the following in mind:

1. Recognize the Golden Cage and Mobius Strip you are in
2. Comprehend your reflection in the form of people, places, things, and experiences.
3. Comprehend your perception knowing all the variables at play.
4. Accept your power as an electrical, crystalline light being.
5. Use intention in everything you do since it's the key to a magnificent life.
6. Avail your inner fire and spark to maximize your momentary experiences.

If even a tiny percentage of humans start vibrating as quantum beings, we can create a very positive ripple effect. The law of cause and effect and the law of conservation of energy are always at work. This phenomenon further explains that what we seek is seeking us. There is "cause and effect" and "cause with effect" simultaneously and instantaneously occurring. As we cause an effect, we create an effect. For example, when we think of someone, they may also be thinking of us. We both are accessing each other's energies at the same time. There is no delay in an energy transfer when living in a quantum universe because thought travels faster than light.

Therefore, each person living with self-responsibility can start their own 100th monkey effect. The compound effect of an empowered group of quantum beings can change the shape of humanity and bring Heaven to Earth.

Being a human craft, we consist of gadgets, crystals, and elements from the periodic table. We have a unique soul signature with a built-in navigation system. Our vibration and frequency direct us to the places on Earth that are calling to us. We are being led to where we need to be.

We humans perceive based on a comparison of data received from both the Right and Left hemispheres and Intrinsic memory. Microtubules enabling our consciousness to drive our will via intention affect our daily manifestation.

The quantum being processing unit is in perpetual existence day in and day out and runs on a feedback loop. If you understand your power, you can take an active role in what inputs you allow, how you process them, and how it shows up daily. Create consciously with your daily actions since God is working through you. Maintaining our spark is accomplished by fleeing the Golden Cage and exiting the Mobius Strip through wisdom and conscious evolution in the perpetual reflective universe.

About Shehnaz Soni

Shehnaz is an accomplished Aerospace Engineer, an Author, an Energy Healer, Health and Transformational Coach, and proud Mother

S hehnaz was born and raised as an orthodox Muslim in Karachi, Pakistan. From day one, she was asked to fit inside a box that didn't align with her true calling. She grew up feeling trapped within a patriarchal, cultural mindset where women are groomed, expected to be wives and homemakers, and not encouraged to go to school. Being a bright and headstrong young girl, she pushed  over one barrier after another in her determination to complete her high school education and go on to college. Shehnaz graduated high school as the valedictorian and continued engineering at the University of Karachi despite persistent cultural and familial abuse and degradation as a female.

Her aspirations to achieve a college degree and financial independence were soon obliterated when obligatory arranged marriage disrupted her education. Dictated by cultural tradition, she was married off to a stranger after a one-hour interview, and quickly after the wedding, she immigrated to the United States with her new groom, leaving everything behind.

Upon her arrival in the United States, she faced a new set of challenges, including financial, cultural, and language barriers—as she tried to acculturate to her new life. In facing the choice to either do what was expected and approved or to expand her inner self, Shehnaz reawakened her trailblazer instincts and chose the path of transformation. Therefore, as a transformational coach, she uses the bio-individuality philosophy, meaning everyone is unique. What is one person's food can be another person's poison. She is certified at the Institute of Integrative Nutrition Health Coach.

Committed to pursuing her dream life, she attended a community college to learn English. She already spoke three languages – Urdu, Gujarati (goo-jar-a-tee), and Hindi but had long-dreamed of speaking English fluently. Her decision not to take "no" for an answer rewarded her with a degree in electrical engineering at the University of California, Irvine. This achievement launched her into a life of financial independence, space exploration, and an ongoing personal expedition of change at both the physical and quantum level.

Shehnaz has worked as a rocket scientist for both Boeing and NASA. Her work on the massive rocket called the Space Launch System (SLS) will be used in one of the earlier missions to facilitate living on the Moon. Additionally, she assisted in building and implementing the Falcon 9 rocket which provided taxi service for astronauts aboard the International Space Station eliminating our reliance on the Russian Soyuz rocket.

Her most recent work at NASA includes the Artemis Project. She and her cutting-edge team of aerospace engineers have developed requirements for the unprecedented Human Landing System, also known as HLS. When ready to launch, this system will finally bridge mankind with a long-term presence on the

Moon and ultimately on Mars. The astronauts, preselected to take this flagship journey, will include the first woman and the first person of color ever to step foot on the south side of the Moon and ultimately Mars.

As the author of The Quantum Being, Shehnaz shares her passion through writing. This book is part memoir and part guide for humanity and will bridge science and spirituality to help the reader realize the truth of their magnificence as human beings on the journey to manifest their own miracles.

Shehnaz believes that we all have the power to live an incredible life as quantum beings. She teaches Quantum Physics implementation in daily life to heal and reprogram un-serving beliefs and patterns. Through her group workshops and sessions as a health and Transformation Coach, she shares her knowledge and experience to guide clients and students toward enlightenment and self-empowerment in all aspects of their lives. Being a quantum human, she believes, is to embark on an alchemical transformation toward our highest life potential.

Shehnaz's quest of understanding life force energy has provided here with the following credentials as an Energy Healer:

1. Certified Life Activation Practitioner – King Solomon Lineage at the Modern Mystery School.
2. Certified Access Consciousness Bars Healer
3. Certified Reiki Level II

She is a BEMER Distributor - A Bioelectromagnetic Energy regulation machine that enhances microcirculation. She also provides one-on-one healing sessions using crystal, or sound healing as necessary to bring a moment of clarity to lifelong questions about how we fin into the greater scheme of things by turning on our spiritual DNA, divine blueprint so that we begin to awaken and remember our highest potential.

As we undertake the daunting task of transformation, we embark on the journey that will ultimately become habitual, automatic, and effortless – akin to a rocket leaving the Earth. At first, the initial launch requires enormous power, then less and less as it leaves the Earth's gravitational field. Finally, the rocket moves through space under its own momentum breaking all the barriers, beyond imagination to traverse new worlds.

Glossary

Aether: The aether or ether is an ever-present field that connects all things.

Akashic record: A compendium of all events, thoughts, actions, and feelings that have occurred throughout time and throughout our existence. This is a universal database.

Alchemy: The ancient study and philosophy of how to change basic substances such as metals into other substances. Self-Transformation through conscious evolution.

Atomic: Forming a single, irreducible component in a larger system.

Bifurcation: The point at which something divides into two branches or parts.

Chakra: Means "wheel" in Sanskrit and refers to energy points in our body.

Covidiocy: Implies only in today's society could we coin a modern term to describe the ignorance that comes from continually questioning what we believe to be our truth.

Craft: A vehicle designed to move you through space, such as a boat, plane, space shuttle, or even the human body.

Crown Chakra: The "wheel" of energy located at the top (crown) of the head.

Dimensions: Dimensions are a spacetime operating framework creating a foundation for the perception we operate from. If you are in a 2-dimensional operating space you can't comprehend, how can you imagine a third or fourth dimension? We must transcend dimensions beyond spacetime.

Fibonacci sequence: The representation of fractality in nature through a number sequence that is naturally occurring.

Golden ratio or golden mean: The divine proportion in mathematics that is naturally occurring.

Hologram: A hologram is a three-dimensional projection in the form of a waveform created with a photographic recording of a light field due to diffraction (interference).

Intelligent architecture: The weaving material that interconnects all things visible-physical and invisible-nonphysical.

Kabbalah: An ancient knowledge system initially passed down by Metatron, Prophet Ibrahim, and ultimately adapted by Rabi, generally connected to the Jewish religion. The meaning of Kabbalah is to receive light, where light is energy and energy is information to transcend God within us. Kabbalah teaching explains how energy transforms into matter.

Karma: Newton's Third Law of Motion. For every cause, there is an effect. These effects ultimately impact everyone.

Kundalini energy: Energy intertwined in our spine, signifying the duality within us.

Mandelbrot set: The Mandelbrot Set is the depiction of mathematical patterns that occur in a number of natural systems.

Manifestation: To bring dreams and desires into being through embodiment.

Maya: The Sanskrit word for illusion.

Metaphysics: The branch of philosophy that deals with abstract concepts that are beyond classical physics. This is where we dwell in all non-physical aspects of our existence.

Macrocosm and Microcosm: The macrocosm is the world as a whole, with a microcosm being one small part, often humankind, taken as a model. One encompasses the other and keeps folding into fractal worlds of its own, like Russian Dolls.

Morphogenetic field: Invisible pattern-forming agents that guide the biological process of development. A field that shapes the morphogenesis of objects much like a magnetic field would do to iron filings. This field is connected with the Akashic field, where Akashic records are stored.

Piezoelectricity: A process that turns mechanical energy into electrical energy.

Quantum: The smallest discrete amount of energy.

Sacred geometry: The geometric forms beautifully choreographed by nature.

Self-similarity: Exhibiting similar patterns at increasingly smaller scales; also known as the expanding or unfolding symmetry we see in the fractals and human design.

Sigil: An intention-charged symbol of a desired goal.

Sinusoidal wave: The most natural representation of how things in nature change state.

Superposition: Superposition is the ability of a quantum system to be in multiple states at the same time until it is measured.

Synchronicity: The simultaneous occurrence of events that appear significantly related as a message from the universe across time and space.

Universal constants: Numbers used for pattern identification.

NOTE: These definitions are my interpretations of these words.

Bibliography

ii *100th Monkey Effect*, https://100monkey.co.uk/project/100th-monkey-effect-explained/

iii Global Heart, *The Seven Essene Mirrors*, https://globalheart.nl/spiritualiteit/the-seven-essene-mirrors/

iv David R. Hawkins, M.D., Ph.D., *The Map of Consciousness Explained*, https://www.amazon.com/Map-Consciousness-Explained-Actualize-Potential/dp/1401959644#:~:text=With%20the%20Map%2C%20Dr.,Ecstasy%2C%20Peace%2C%20and%20Enlightenment

v Emma Tuzzio, The Muse in the Mirror, *Cymatics: Making Sound Visible*, https://themuseinthemirror.com/2014/11/29/cymatics-making-sound-visible/

vi Dr. Emoto, *What the Bleep Do We Know*, (Water Experiment), https://whatthebleep.com/water-crystals/

vii Philip Gardiner, Max Napolitano, Richard Pitt, *Absolute Magick*, Documentary on Amazon Prime, Video, https://www.amazon.com/Absolute-Magick-Exposed-Philip-Gardiner/dp/B01BE8OHAK/ref=sr_1_1?crid=DELI6P8ZK2CK&keywords=absolute+magick&qid=1659055154&s=instant-video&sprefix=absolute+magick%2Cinstant-video%2C171&sr=1-1

viii Quantum University, *What Are Morphogenetic Fields?* https://youtu.be/GEdPpEDP9X4

ix Philip Gardiner, Max Napolitano, Richard Pitt, *Absolute Magick*, Documentary on Amazon Prime, Video, https://www.amazon.com/Absolute-Magick-Exposed-Philip-Gardiner/dp/B01BE8OHAK/ref=sr_1_1?crid=DELI6P8ZK2CK&keywords=absolute+magick&qid=1659055154&s=instant-video&sprefix=absolute+magick%2Cinstant-video%2C171&sr=1-1

x Quantum Gravity Research, *Home of Emergence Theory*, https://quantumgravityresearch.org/, *Hacking Our Reality: E8 Theory (Official)*, https://youtu.be/vGZ9poT2qH4, *Emergence Theory: A Layperson's Guide* https://youtu.be/Qa4JkgKDaR0

BIBLIOGRAPHY

[xi] Klee Irwin, *The Tetrahedron*, https://youtu.be/xTN9tQGgN6Q

[xii] Sebastian Anthony, Extreme Tech, *Harvard cracks DNA storage, crams 700 terabytes of data into a single gram*, Harvard cracks DNA storage, crams 700 terabytes of data into a single gram - ExtremeTech

[xiii] Nassim Haramein, *Flower of Life*, https://youtu.be/lymI67Y90m8

[xiv] Tom Huston, *Finding Spirit in the Fabric of Space and Time, An Exploration of Quantum Consciousness with Dr. Stuart Hameroff, MD*, http://tomhuston. com/portfolio/quantum.html, Dr. Stuart Hammerof, *Quantum Physics of Consciousness*, https://youtu.be/gfmcEbD64XY

[xv] Spirit Science 6, *The Ancient Secret of the Flower of Life*, https://youtu.be/ RHuvW7YaGjQ

[xvi] Michael Schirber, Life Science, *The Chemistry of Life: The Human Body* (Human and Periodic Table), https://www.livescience.com/3505-chemistry-life-human-body.html

[xvii] Kristen Houser, *Alien Among Us*, https://futurism.com/the-byte/astrobiologist-invisible-aliens-live-earth

[xviii] Charles Q. Choi, Live Science, *Strange! Humans Glow in Visible Light*, https://www.livescience.com/7799-strange-humans-glow-visible-light.html

[xix] Olivia Bader-Lee on the results of the University of Bielefeld study, Germany *Science Confirms That People Absorb Energy From Others*, https://www.theoneminutemiracleinc.com/blogs/people-absorb-positive-energy/science-confirms-that-people-absorb-energy-from-science-confirms-that-people-absorb-energy-from-others

[xx] John Riehl, *The Roots of Human Self-Awareness*, University of Iowa brain study, https://now.uiowa.edu/2012/08/roots-human-self-awareness

[xxi] Tom Huston, *Finding Spirit in the Fabric of Space and Time, An Exploration of Quantum Consciousness with Dr. Stuart Hameroff, MD*, http://tomhuston. com/portfolio/quantum.html, Dr. Stuart Hammerof, *Quantum Physics of Consciousness*, https://youtu.be/gfmcEbD64XY

[xxii] Roger Penrose Webinar 2021, https://youtu.be/gLUEw-EU8kk, Sir Roger Penrose, *Why Explore Cosmos and Consciousness?* https://youtu.be/dlv8DVb6e0Q

[xxiii] John Riehl, *The Roots of Human Self-Awareness*, University of Iowa brain study, https://now.uiowa.edu/2012/08/roots-human-self-awareness

xxiv Tom Huston, *Finding Spirit in the Fabric of Space and Time, An Exploration of Quantum Consciousness with Dr. Stuart Hameroff, MD,* http://tomhuston.com/portfolio/quantum.html, Dr. Stuart Hammerof, *Quantum Physics of Consciousness,* https://youtu.be/gfmcEbD64XY

xxv *The Primacy of Consciousness,* Peter Russell Interview, https://youtu.be/-d4ugppcRUE

xxvi *CIA Declassified: Holographic universe (The Consciousness Matrix),* CIA paper on Gateway Process dated 1983 and work of Itzhak Bentov, The Gateway Process CIA Hemi Sync, CIA-RDP96-00788R001700210016-5.pdf, https://youtu.be/bOYl1oqgDX4

xxvii Peter Fenwick, *What Really Happens When You Die,* Studies of End-of-Life Phenomena, Death Study, https://www.youtube.com/watch?v=aiEYQyUjAQA&ab_channel=ThanatosTVEN

xxviii Frank Echenhofer, Chronicles 1, *How Does Ayahuasca Affect Consciousness?* https://www.youtube.com/watch?v=tbOj9RIH-GU&ab_channel=ConsciousPictures

xxix Alexandra Witze, Nature.com, *Astronaut Twins Study Spots Subtle Genetic Changes Caused by Space Travel,* https://www.nature.com/articles/d41586-019-01149-y

xxx Roger Penrose Webinar 2021, https://youtu.be/gLUEw-EU8kk, Sir Roger Penrose, *Why Explore Cosmos and Consciousness?* https://youtu.be/dlv8DVb6e0Q

xxxi Tom Huston, *Finding Spirit in the Fabric of Space and Time, An Exploration of Quantum Consciousness with Dr. Stuart Hameroff, MD,* http://tomhuston.com/portfolio/quantum.html, Dr. Stuart Hammerof, *Quantum Physics of Consciousness,* https://youtu.be/gfmcEbD64XY

xxxii Roger Penrose Webinar 2021, https://youtu.be/gLUEw-EU8kk, Sir Roger Penrose, *Why Explore Cosmos and Consciousness?* https://youtu.be/dlv8DVb6e0Q

xxxiii University of California Irvine, Interview, *Prof. Donald Hoffman, The Case Against Reality: On Conscious Agent Theory,* https://youtu.be/dd6CQCbk2ro

xxxiv Medha Chandorkar, Mic.com, *9 Mind-Blowing Facts About Voyager 1,* https://www.mic.com/articles/54035/9-mind-blowing-facts-about-voyager-1

xxxv Lynn McTaggart, *The Leaf Intention Experiment,* https://lynnemctaggart.com/the-leaf-intention-experiment/

BIBLIOGRAPHY

[xxxvi] Ross Pomeroy, Real Clear Science, *Why Is There Magnetite in the Human Brain?* https://www.realclearscience.com/blog/2019/06/11/why_is_there_magnetite_in_the_human_brain.html

[xxxvii] Ben Thomas, Discover Magazine, *The Man Who Tried to Weigh the Soul,* https://www.discovermagazine.com/mind/the-man-who-tried-to-weigh-the-soul

[xxxviii] Dr. Adrian Owen, *Detecting Consciousness: A Unique Role for Neuroimaging,* https://www.uwo.ca/bmi/owenlab/pdf/2013-Owen,%20Annual%20Review%20-%20Detecting%20consciousness%20A%20role%20for%20neuroimaging.pdf

[xxxix] Tom Huston, *Finding Spirit in the Fabric of Space and Time, An Exploration of Quantum Consciousness with Dr. Stuart Hameroff, MD,* http://tomhuston.com/portfolio/quantum.html, Dr. Stuart Hammerof, *Quantum Physics of Consciousness,* https://youtu.be/gfmcEbD64XY

[xl] Peter Fenwick, *What Really Happens When You Die,* Studies of End-of-Life Phenomena, Death Study, https://www.youtube.com/watch?v=aiEYQyUjAQA&ab_channel=ThanatosTVEN

[xli] Tom Huston, *Finding Spirit in the Fabric of Space and Time, An Exploration of Quantum Consciousness with Dr. Stuart Hameroff, MD,* http://tomhuston.com/portfolio/quantum.html, Dr. Stuart Hammerof, *Quantum Physics of Consciousness,* https://youtu.be/gfmcEbD64XY

[xlii] *Babylon 5: Minbari Philosophy,* T.V. series, https://youtu.be/2jzMTImdBVI

[xliii] Chad Orzel, *Schrödinger's cat: A thought experiment in quantum mechanics,* https://youtu.be/UjaAxUO6-Uw

Made in United States
North Haven, CT
13 October 2022

25404047R00166